What others are saying about *Writing Exceptional Missionary Newsletters*:

"This book is a 'must read' for all missionaries who want to communicate effectively with their prayer and donor support teams. It is packed with practical ideas and examples. I have already used many of the lessons from this book, which has become my reference 'Bible' in writing prayer letters."

—Bob Reehm, Veteran Navigator Staff and Author

"For seven years, I served as Senior Pastor to a church that sponsored 16 missionaries. Some of their newsletters garnered little attention; others gripped my heart. This book shows how to capture the reader's heart. It is necessary for any missionary seeking to cultivate a broad and effective support base, and multiply his or her work for the Kingdom of God."

—Roger VanDerWerken, U.S. Navy Chaplain and Author

"This book stirred my motivation for effective communication and gave practical helps. I recently used two of the ideas in an appeal letter and God brought a 75 percent increase in funds!"

—Mike Schmid, National Associate Military Director for The Navigators

"Sometimes people lose interest in a ministry because of meager newsletters. Sandy brings a fresh and visual approach to help mission workers improve how they communicate on paper. Easy step-by-step processes, quality examples, helpful checklists, and fun anecdotes make this book necessary for any communicator."

—Rev. Skip Taylor, Training Director for International Christian Ministries

Writing Exceptional Missionary Newsletters

Essentials for writing, producing and sending
newsletters that motivate readers

by Sandy Weyeneth

William Carey Library
Pasadena, California
www.WCLBooks.com

Writing Exceptional Missionary Newsletters

Published by:
William Carey Library
P.O. Box 40129
Pasadena, California 91114
www.WCLBooks.com

Cover Artist: Soulfisher Designs

Printed in the United States of America

ISBN: 0-87808-455-X

CONTENTS

Chapter Four – Sending and Mailing Essentials

Chapter Five – E-Mail and Personal Websites

Chapter Six – Sending Newsletters While Living Overseas

Chapter Seven – Final Thoughts
One thing may help you the most

APPENDIX

RESOURCES

Acknowledgements

I wish to thank several friends who made this book possible.

To those who taught me about great writing: Glenn Balsis, Becky Brodin, Janet Dunn, and Scott Morton in particular. I'll never forget when Janet "red-penned" one of my first newsletters when I was in my early twenties. I thought, "I just wanted you to look at it, not rewrite it!" But she was right, and I learned much in the arduous process of becoming a better communicator. Janet, Scott, Becky and Glenn have been patient, practical, and wonderfully encouraging. I admire their talent and heart. All are tremendous friends, colleagues, and mentors.

Thanks also to Carrie Coffman who mentored me through her terrific book on newsletters.

Much appreciation and thanks to several friends who gave me excellent and valuable feedback: Coleen Harvey, Mike Gerhard, Roger VanDerWerken, Susan Nikaido, Becky Brodin, Glenn Balsis, Peter Udall, Scott Morton, Bob Reehm, Mike Schmid, Skip Taylor, and my husband Randy. Your insights helped make these ideas and information useable. I appreciate it!

Thank you to friends and great communicators who took time to review my manuscript and endorse it: Jerry Bridges, Scott Morton, Bob Reehm, Jerry White, Roger VanDerWerken, Mike Schmid, and Skip Taylor. I am grateful.

Thank you to many friends and colleagues who let me use your newsletters as examples. Your writing inspires and shows excellent technique.

Finally, thank you Lord Jesus Christ for giving me and other missionaries the ministry stories to write about. This book is written to bring honor and glory toYour name.

Dedication

To Randy my husband and partner, whose love overwhelms me. From day one of mentioning that I would like to create this book, you have been enthusiastic and supportive.

You are a terrific friend, partner, and husband, and I am enjoying all that God has for us in life and ministry.

Here are definitions for terms and icons used throughout the book.

Newsletter: Letter to your whole mailing list giving ministry stories, news, updates, and prayer requests. It is also referred to as a prayer letter.

Fundraising Letter: Letter with the purpose to ask for a financial gift for ministry.

Donor: Someone who financially supports your ministry with regular or periodic gifts.

Donor Letter: Letter to just those who financially support your ministry on a regular basis. It is separate from a newsletter, less formal, and gives further ministry updates, answers to prayer, prayer requests, and personal news.

A good idea to apply.

Introduction

Too many boring and dull missionary newsletters get sent. No doubt you have received a few. They are too long or overcrowded. Others have buckets of data, but little passion. Yet every once in a while, a fantastic newsletter captures your heart. It reads like a good book you can't put down. What's the secret?

In my role with The Navigators' Staff Funding Team, I coached hundreds of veteran and new missionaries to write top-notch newsletters. While editing, I noticed a pattern of mistakes and missed opportunities. I wondered, "Why isn't there a book that demonstrates how to write exceptional missionary newsletters and features guidelines on the whole newsletter process?"

This book is the result. It covers common errors found in typical newsletters and offers proven tips guaranteed to enrich your writing. It will assist you in your efforts to help fulfill Jesus Christ's Great Commission in Matthew 28:18-20, "Go therefore and make disciples of all the nations...."

It also presents solutions and ideas on non-writing issues. Not long ago I dreaded sending my newsletter because of the hours demanded to write 400 personal notes. A mentor gave a marvelous solution. This book spells out that solution and dozens of others.

Few missionaries become missionaries because they want to write letters, however that does not make newsletters a necessary evil. The New Testament is, in fact, full of follow-up letters to Christians from missionaries. Communicating *is* what missionaries do; therefore your newsletter *is* ministry too!

If you follow the suggestions offered in this book, the production and sending of your newsletter will bring more satisfaction and joy to you, and your readers will enjoy reading it! It will also benefit church mission committee members, pastors, mission leaders—anyone who helps missionaries with their prayer letters.

Whether this is your first or fiftieth newsletter, my hope is that you:

- Apply these ideas.
- Communicate regularly and view your newsletter as the primary way you represent your mission work to others.
- Live out Colossians 4:6 (my paraphrase), "Let your newsletters be always full of grace, seasoned with Tabasco sauce."

Don't settle for mediocre when captivating is possible. The Lord Jesus Christ will be honored, and your readers will appreciate it so much that they will want to read more, pray more, be involved more, and give more.

Thank you for your wonderful work and service. I invite you to jump in and discover how these practical ideas will boost your writing so that your readers can't put it down!

PART I – ESSENTIALS FOR WRITING NEWSLETTERS

Her comment shocked me.

A young missionary repeated her supervisor's opinion of newsletters: "It doesn't matter so much what you say, just as long as you get out some information."

Another friend's note sobered me: "I have supported Brian (not real name) for eighteen months. I got one thank you from him initially, but I have heard nothing from him since. I don't know what is happening in his ministry. I am sorry but I have decided to stop my support."

Unfortunately, these situations may not be uncommon. A view that "getting out a newsletter" is more important than the content of the letter is like saying: "It doesn't matter what you say to your stockholders, just bang out a letter." Or Brian's view of not sending out a newsletter for over a year is like saying, "You helped pay for me to be on campus and minister, but I don't have time to tell you what is going on."

My goal is to fuel your commitment to communicate and to ignite your ability to communicate well. Part I offers compelling reasons to send newsletters and ways to write exceptional ones.

Chapter One - Why Write a Newsletter?

An actual sign seen across the good ol' USA:
On a long-established New Mexico dry cleaners: *"38 years on the same spot."*

Who has time to write a newsletter? Ministry is hectic. Life hardly slows down. When newsletter time comes, I think, "Again already? Didn't we just send one out?" Then I snap back to reality, and I remember John's story.

John told me how the missions committee for his church decided which of three new missionaries to support. After discussion, one fifty year-old businessman cast the deciding vote, "Let's support Todd and Alicia because we know we will hear from them. We've already received a few letters from them."

Wow. No rocket science there. That should seal my resolve to send newsletters! Yet a thought *still* pesters me now and then: Is sending a newsletter really worth all of the effort?

What do you think? Formulate your response and list three benefits a missionary receives in sending out a newsletter.

A. _____

B. _____

C. _____

Missionaries from over ten different mission groups gave these compelling benefits for writing newsletters:

❶ Newsletters generate prayer.

A missionary from Indiana wrote:

"Several months ago, I visited a college friend Jon whom I had not talked to in ten years. During those years, I had faithfully sent he and his wife my newsletters, but I heard nothing from them. When I saw their refrigerator, I almost cried. There was a picture of me from my Kenya mission's trip almost eight years ago! They had prayed for me faithfully for that trip and for all these years!"

<u>The more people hear from you, the more they will likely pray</u>. It's that simple. In today's busy world, all of us need reminders. Newsletters are tangible reminders.

❷ Newsletters show what God is doing.

Friends want to know your challenges, the barriers to the Gospel, and the praises and successes of your ministry. This reminds me of Proverbs 15:23, "A man has joy in an apt answer, and how delightful is a timely word!" They want to feel your ministry, weep with you, and rejoice with you. You have some of the most exciting stories around!

❸ Newsletters illustrate the ministry and inspire continued financial support.

> Ignore your teeth and they will go away.

So proclaimed a Wisconsin Dental Association billboard. Likewise, if you ignore your donors (financial supporters), they will go away. Consider these examples of why people stopped supporting a missionary:

> After my first gift a year ago, I received a letter from them. I have never received a letter expressing gratitude, or explaining how God is using them, or detailing their plans, or requesting prayer since.
>
> If I don't receive some regular communications, I'll have to stop my support. I must give where I believe it will do the most good. Hopefully I'll hear from them soon.

I asked friends, **"Have you ever stopped giving to a missionary? If so, why?"**

> "We give regularly to a couple of dozen people, but we rarely hear from them. It's sad. It seems gratefulness is not part of their make-up. We ask, 'Why bother giving to them?'"

> "I supported a fellow staff for 12 months. I never heard any thank you from him so I stopped giving."

It's not rocket science. People have several choices of where to invest their money. We do not communicate simply for the income streams, but the more we keep in touch with our donor team, the more likely they will keep giving. Expect some attrition in your support base, but do not let your lack of communication be the culprit!

Long-time missionaries John and Helen understood Matthew 6:21, "...for where your treasure is, there will your heart be also." They love people and know that people often give to what touches their hearts. John says,

> "Personal, consistent contact is one of the best ways to keep donor support. In fact, we have about a dozen friends who have supported us consistently since 1958! Staying in contact through letters has been a key."

❹ Newsletters offer ministry ideas.

Ministry ideas featured in your newsletters have outstanding potential to reproduce.

- Tony likes your evangelism idea and tries it.
- Danielle is intrigued by your story of personally helping someone grow in Christ and decides to disciple Jackie.
- Jose and Maria replicate your idea to serve your neighbors as part of an outreach for Christ.

Peter, a missionary colleague, inspired me with his attitude:

> "I view my mailing list as an important ministry audience, just like I would students on a campus, military staff on a base, and so on. My mindset is to minister to people who read my letters like I would to an audience I was preparing a talk for, or a Bible study I was leading. I ask God to inspire them about missions and to discover ministry ideas and tools they can practice. They may only perceive my letters as updates, but I seek to minister and bless those I write to with stories and ideas they might be able to apply to their own lives and ministry."

❺ Newsletters broaden exposure to missions.

In *How to Write Missionary Letters,* Alvera Mickelsen explains, "Missionaries can exert influence on the perceptions of the Christian public and especially on pastors and mission-minded people in the local church. The letters you write may be the only contact your readers have with missions and missionaries."

When 28 year-old Marie read missionary newsletters for six years and visited with missionaries, she grew burdened for people with little chance of hearing the gospel. Marie eventually journeyed half way around the world to take the good news of Christ to another culture!

❻ Newsletters communicate thanks.

Everyone enjoys hearing "thank you." In your newsletter, be sure and say it. It can sound something like:

"Thank you for your prayers and support for this ministry. It means a lot."

"We appreciate you and value your partnership."

"Thanks for standing with us in this ministry of changing lives."

> "You need to decide that expressing appreciation will be part of your ministry."
> —William Dillon, *People Raising*

Newsletters extend and strengthen your relationship with others. Friendships dwindle without communication and deepen with communication. In like manner, your newsletter extends your heart and love and appreciation.

See page 117 for *Fifty Ways of Saying "Thank You" to your giving partners.*

Include fellow missionaries who support you as donors.

Some missionaries mistakenly think, "Cindy (a fellow missionary) understands living on support. She knows we are thankful for her monthly support. She understands we are trying to save money, so I do not need to thank her or send her our support team letters."

That is a false assumption. Send fellow missionaries like Cindy thank-you letters and include them as regular donors. The ways that you express gratitude to your regular donors get expressed to Cindy as well. The same holds true for family members who are donors.

Chapter Two –Tips for Excellent Writing

You want friends to dig in and read your newsletter right away, not simply glance at it. Apply the following eight tips to your next newsletter and it will burst with pizzazz and capture your reader's interest. The tips are illustrated in the following newsletter model and explained in subsequent chapters.

MISSIONARY NEWSLETTER MODEL

THE NAVIGATORS

Jesus? – Resurrection?   Unbelievable! – Unbelievable!

October 26, 2001

Dear Friends,

Yoshi was obviously not convinced that Jesus had risen from the dead. But now he is! Yoshi came to Christ about 6 months ago.

It was Friday afternoon on a beautiful September Colorado day. The room was buzzing with conversation. Forty-two new and veteran missionaries were paired in twos and stories were flying as I called the group back to order.

We were wrestling with a topic of utmost interest to the 27 new missionaries. The topic – *How to explain their ministries to friends and churches.* The best way to understand someone's ministry would be to visit and see it in action. In 1995 I visited several of the missionaries I had trained in Russia – I understood like never before what their ministry was all about.

Unfortunately, our new missionaries can't take most of their friends to their ministry locations. So what's the best alternative? Tell a **good story** that will paint a **verbal picture** of what it's like to be a missionary.

I asked who had a good story about ministry. Steven stood and told us about Yoshi, who he had met the previous summer in Japan. Yoshi, like most Japanese, knew little about Jesus. He had however, been hanging around several of the Navigators in his city.

Left to right: Tom, <u>Steven</u> & Bryan will minis... in Japan. Nic is on his way to South Africa.

Steven was visiting Yoshi's city on a summer mission's trip. One day Yoshi, Steven and Cory, another believer from the U.S., were in a friend's apartment. Yoshi noticed the word **gospel** on a piece of literature and asked what it meant. After a lengthy discussion Yoshi turned to Cory and asked, "Cory, do you believe Jesus – resurrection?"

As Yoshi asked his question he held one forearm parallel to the ground and as he said "resurrection" he rotated his arm at the elbow until his fingers pointed straight up. Cory copied Yoshi's arm gestured and said that yes, he believed Jesus – resurrection. Yoshi then turned to Steven and repeated the same question with the same arm gesture. Steven duplicated Cory's response.

After a pregnant pause Steven asked Yoshi the obvious question. "Yoshi, how about you? Do you believe Jesus – resurrection? Yoshi, with a frown on his face pondered for a minute, rotated his arm upward again, shook his head no and then responded. "Jesus – resurrection? UNBELIEVABLE! – UNBELIEVABLE!"

MISSIONARY NEWSLETTER MODEL continued

Steven went on to tell us that 6 months later Yoshi came to believe in Christ as his Savior. Yoshi is growing in his faith as our Navigator missionaries are helping him. Steven is returning to Japan so he can help reach and disciple others like Yoshi.

Ten minutes into writing this letter, I received a phone call from Mike, a new staff with the Navs who's reaching students at an Ivy League university. (I'd helped Mike and his wife as they raised their financial support last year.) Mike's leading two discussion groups with atheists and skeptics in the freshman dorms. Monday nights and again on Thursdays he heads up the hill to campus with several liters of soda and 3 large pizzas. He arrives about 30 minutes before the discussion and begins to knock on the doors of students who've been at previous discussions.

Tip 6: Write with vitality.

The first week the kids dug into the pizza and Mike threw out a quote from Dostoevsky's book, The Brothers Karamazov. The main topic was, If God doesn't exist does it matter how we live – morally? The discussion was fast and furious, as all the students wanted to share their views. Each discussion began with 6 students. Now 3 weeks later, both groups have grown to 13-17 students.

Adam is a Christian student who's hosting one of the discussions in his suite. Evan, Adam's non-Christian roommate, wanted to attend as well. However, when the first discussion rolled around Evan had plans to "party hard" that evening. Since the discussion would be over by 10:45, Mike convinced Evan to stay for the discussion and party afterwards. Not only did Evan stay but so did his two buddies who came to pick him up at 10:00.

Tip 7: Personalize it. Sign each letter with a color other than black. This small investment is worth it!

The next week Evan showed up again. So did his two buddies and they also brought another friend! That's how God is working. Students are coming out of the woodwork to get in on these discussions. After 6 weeks of discussions on philosophical topics, Mike will invite these freshmen to investigate the Gospel of John with him. Wouldn't you love to be a fly on the wall during those discussions? (By the way, Mike has his PHD in Philosophy so he's holding his own during the discussions!)

After 9 years of training new missionaries, I still get excited about helping folks like Mike and Steven. I know that once their funding is in place they will reach people like Yoshi and Evan all around the world!

Thanks again for your partnership as I help Mike, Steven and scores of other new missionaries. Our world needs all the missionaries we can get these days!

In Christ,

Bob Seibert

Bob Seibert

Tip 8: Get feedback on your letter before printing it.

Name, address, logo

Include your first and last name, address and logo.

Tip 1: INCLUDE A STORY

> Printed in a church bulletin:
> *"The sermon this morning: Jesus Walks on the Water."*
> *"The sermon tonight: Searching for Jesus."*

Consider last Sunday's sermon. What did your pastor preach about? Most people I ask respond something like: "I don't remember, but I recall the story he told about the high school teacher who saved a student's life."

We remember stories. They engage the heart and mind. Prison Fellowship founder Charles Colson talked to a man who theorized that the next Billy Graham will be a playwright (Colson 2002). If this man is right, Colson adds, "…it's because moral propositions are absorbed much more easily through images and the medium of storytelling than through dry, theological treatises. Stories shape our thoughts, move our emotions and enlarge our imaginations."

Stories stick. They powerfully communicate truth, ideas and events. That is why featuring a short story in your newsletter is the number one way to captivate your readers.

Jesus Christ knew the power of a story. In Matthew 13:10-13, the disciples asked Jesus, "Why do you tell stories?" He replied, "That's why I tell stories: to create readiness, to nudge the people toward receptive insight." *(The Message)*

Jesus could have said, "God forgives your sins, so you also forgive others' sins." Instead he spun the story of the unmerciful servant (Matthew 18:23-35).

A Campus Crusade missionary said it well, "It is not the statistical reports or the ministry updates that excite my ministry partners, but it's the stories behind the statistics that grab their attention. Talk about a life which represents that statistic or report."

Friends do not give funds simply to get you up to budget. They want to invest in changed lives; they want "bang for their buck." Succinct "war stories" (ministry stories) powerfully communicate changed lives.

STORY GUIDELINES TO ENGAGE READERS

1. Keep it short.

In general, a maximum of one to five paragraphs works well for a newsletter story. The following two newsletters illustrate this point.

> "Missionaries tend to make two kinds of errors in their prayer letters. The first is to say too much. The second is to say too little."
> —Glenn Hoyle, *Evangelical Missions Quarterly*

Example of a newsletter story. Jot down what makes this unique story terrific.

_____

_____

Bringing Hope to Missionaries

I enjoy my role as coach and counselor to Navigator staff missionaries as they raise their financial and prayer support. This is a critical area for all missionaries. I had the privilege of helping several staff in the early 1990s and am glad to be at it again.

Glenn was one of the staff I coached. He was at the University of Illinois leading collegiates to Christ and discipling them. Currently, he leads the ministry at the U.S. Air Force Academy in Colorado Springs and is thriving. I pass on his story to give you a feel for the impact this specialized ministry can have…

"I begged not to go to the Fundraising School. Although I had been on Navigator staff for 13 years, our funding was awful. There were incredible tensions because of our low funding. My ministry supervisor insisted that I attend and I came dragging my feet. Mike was my 'coach' during that school. Mike patiently reviewed our personal and ministry budget. Immersed in ministry, I paid little attention to our finances or planning for our future.

One instant discovery was that we were overspending our income each month. Mike showed me that if we were to continue to minister we would need to raise additional funds to cover growing ministry expenses. No one had ever given me this much help before in this difficult area. For some reason Mike's coaching seemed to stick. Like seeing a light at the end of the tunnel, I began to understand my need to raise finances.

Mike's ministry to me didn't stop at the school. He called me at least twice a week to check on how I was doing on raising our funds. There were times I was euphoric with excitement about how God was working. About halfway through the goal my enthusiasm dried up. Mike encouraged me to keep trusting God, and keep making financial appeal appointments. After a ten-week period I was fully funded for the first time on Navigator staff. Without his individual concern and coaching, **I know I wouldn't be ministering today.** *He helped me through the maze of understanding finances, and then personally helped me through the obstacles of raising the needed funds."*

I get my children off to school then wonder what to do with a moment of my own time. My husband is deployed to Norway for training for a month. So, "What is it like being a Christian woman and a military wife?" Well, without the first, I never would be the second. I met Jim in our high school Christian club and knew he planned to join the military. I hoped for six years he would change his mind and get out, but here we are married for ten years. Did I know what I was getting into? Yes and no.

My dad served as a Marine, so I had heard about the perils and trials of the military life. Knowing this, what woman would choose to place herself a whole country away from loving family and friends? Who wants to endure not knowing if the man you love will return alive from his "business trip" to Korea, Afghanistan, or a special training exercise? Who would marry a man who thinks camouflage green is a "cool" color and wears it everyday without complaint? Those are the things I thought of then, now I would add: Who would willingly be a single mother for six or more months at a time? Who would say to their husbands, "Go volunteer to put yourself in the line of fire?" Why would any woman say, "Sure honey more years of moving from base to base would be great living?" Yet, I have said and done all of these things.

No I am not a fool; but I am a woman of God living with the attitude that my vote has been given to God. My desires are in His hands and He knows my dreams and thoughts. My heart often cries out and I often cry, but never has there been a time when my Lord didn't reply. It sometimes comes from a verse long memorized, a worship song, a meaningful hug from a friend, or a one a.m. phone call from my deployed husband. I repeatedly turn to, "My hope is not in this world but in the Lord." And, hope leads to joy and the joy of the Lord never ends.

A military wife by definition is usually independent or must become so rather quickly. She must be made of enduring material that flexes and adapts. For instance, I can change the oil in my car, cut down a Christmas tree, wrestle with my boys, bait a fishing hook, and clean the fish caught. I can work if necessary and have in the past. But, being independent, I have found, means loneliness. The Scripture that comes to me when I am at my lowest or on the way there is, "I will never leave you nor forsake you (Heb 13:5)." Am I independent? Yes, in the eyes of this world I am a liberated woman…but I am dependent on the strength of the Lord.

Being a military Christian wife is incredibly difficult at times. I would not have chosen this path, but I have grown and matured on it. I trust God above all things and I know God is in control of my life and my husbands. So with confidence I can say I have not a clue what will come next, but I will not be alone, broken or destroyed. God is my ROCK and my salvation; whom shall I fear? Certainly not the United States Marine Corps.

2. Help people experience your story first-hand.

While reading C.S. Lewis' *The Chronicles of Narnia* books, I enjoy a "front row seat" watching the main characters Digory, Polly and Aslan. The surprises. The dilemmas. The fears. The elation. It's like I am *right there*. When creating your newsletter, seek to give a similar "front row seat" to your readers. One way is to write draft one when the story and details are fresh and strong in your mind. This allows you to "paint the picture" and shuttle your readers there as if witnessing it first-hand. Don't worry about accuracy yet; just capture the story. Edit it later. Here's how.

Draft One, "Paint the Picture"

One highlight from my summer missions trip to Russia was playing baseball, and it was a fantastic time! The Russian students loved baseball on Saturday mornings. Most of them were brand new at it. Lots of them showed up! I vividly remember Sasha and we became good friends. He had tons of athletic talent and a great sense of humor.

I will not forget when I taught him how to hit. It was very hot, and we were thirsty all the time. We played on an open grassy area at a city park. I was amazed by the potholes in the outfield, little rocks everywhere, and some broken glass around home plate!

I helped Sasha learn to hit the ball. At first he held the bat too vertical and did not bend his knees. He swung hard. After several practice hits, he caught on quickly and loved it. It was obvious that Sasha's confidence grew and he naturally took charge. He coached his teammates on how to play saying, "Run, run!" or "No, go back to the base!"

It was so much fun to see Sasha and the students learn baseball. They loved it! Each Saturday when we played it seemed more and more students showed up, growing to almost 100. I kept trying to teach the fundamentals. It was also hilarious to watch some of the Russian girls on the team play in their dresses and heels! They clapped and went wild when someone scored. We used a softball and there were only three baseball gloves for the whole team! We had no bases initially.

As our friendship grew, I nervously invited Sasha to come to our Bible discussion group. I was excited when he came! Later he said, "We were told at school not to believe in God. But now I see that God is real and I want to learn more. Over the years the school he attended had told him not to believe in God. He has not become a Christian yet but wants to study more of the Bible. That is exciting!

Draft Two, After Editing

"We were told at school not to believe in God. But now I see that God is real and I want to learn more."

Eighteen year-old Sasha told me that this summer!

Thank you for your prayers and support for my mission's trip to Russia. One of the many highlights was the Bible studies and weekend sports activities, baseball in particular. Here is how it began with Sasha.

On a sweltering 95 degree day, 50 eager students walked to the park Saturday morning to play co-ed baseball for the first time. We had three baseball gloves, one softball, two bats, and four cardboard lids for base markers. But mostly, I felt thrilled that Sasha came!

I met Sasha in the dorm where we stayed and invited him to play baseball. Before the game, I pitched for him to hit the ball. At first he held the bat too vertical and his knees stayed stiff. He swung ferociously. But he learned quickly and his confidence soared.

Enthusiasm swelled and Sasha took charge of his team. Sasha coached his beginner teammates and yelled, "Run, run!" or "No, go back to the base!"

What fun to teach Sasha and these enthusiastic students. Eventually, over 100 students showed up! The Russian girls on the team also hit the ball, ran the bases, and dodged numerous potholes in the outfield—all while wearing dresses and high heels! When anyone scored, there was wild clapping and jumping up and down.

Activities like baseball strengthened my friendship with Sasha. After a couple of weeks, I mustered up courage and asked, "Sasha, would you come Tuesday night to a discussion in the dorm about life issues and the Bible?" After five discussions, Sasha was beginning to truly believe in God.

3. Major on ministry and minor on family.

Reading one newsletter I thought, "All they write about is their children. I don't know what is happening in their ministry."

Be careful that family updates do not become the main story in each newsletter. That can happen if we overestimate other's interest in the details of our children's lives. Write about the people your mission serves. People love you and want to hear about your family, but most of your supporters want and deserve to hear what God is doing in the lives of the people to whom you have been sent. Regularly highlight stories from your ministry.

Ideas for family updates:

A. Focus one newsletter a year on family updates.

B. Select a place in your newsletter for occasional and brief updates, important family events, etc.

C. Use a Postscript (P.S.) to write a sentence or two update. For example: "P.S. Our son Greg's college graduation is next month. Please pray for a wonderful celebration and that the Lord will lead him to the right job."

   In fact, also consider using a P.S. for an important news item, reminder, or update because postscripts always get read. In our newsletter about discipling a military couple, I added, "P.S. We're also excited to help with the Billy Graham Mission (crusade) in San Diego coming May 8-11. Please pray for miracles and changed lives as we 'ramp up' for it."

D. Add a half page periodically with family news.

4. Change names to protect people if needed.

There may be occasions when you should not use someone's real name in order to protect him or her. Simply give them a different name in your story. If you do use their real name, ask for permission so they won't be surprised when they read it in your newsletter.

5. Be vulnerable.

Talk about how life is, rather than how it ought to be. Be candid. This does not mean you can whine about how hard ministry is or the meager amount of your last paycheck. One missionary in Japan writes honestly and shares his burdens. Each time I get his letter, it moves me to pray. Another missionary from Russia wrote, "I did not want to come to St. Petersburg, Russia and I had a bad attitude when I got here. It arose from disappointment with the way I expected things to be. I asked God almost every day, "Why are we here?"…But oh the blessings and joy God gave me."

Do not be afraid to share a failure, a struggle in evangelism, or a heartache in discipleship. Friends relate to the frustrations of ministry, and they will stand by you in prayer. There is power in open-ended stories. It can be a story that does not end well or one still in process.

6. Try a new tactic.

If you are stuck in writing, try this missionary's suggestion: When you write your story, imagine you write for *Newsweek* or *Time*. Imagine you are in a friendly competition to get your editor to select your story over other correspondents. Beat them.

7. Let someone in your ministry tell his or her story.

You edit it. My husband Randy did an informal interview with one couple we had in Bible study, sort of like *Larry King Live*. In our newsletter, we used a question and answer format. Another missionary asked one of his ministry leaders to describe what he learned about evangelism that year. Yet another asked a new believer to tell how she came to Christ. It was powerful, like an "inside story." Our donors frequently comment positively on our letters when others tell their story.

Jot down who you could ask to tell their story.

 Ask your ministry supervisor to write a paragraph or a couple of sentences that endorse you and your ministry. Include it as part of your letter. It is potent when someone else applauds you and your efforts. Proverbs 27:2 says, "Let another praise you, and not your own mouth...."

8. Do not preach.

A church staff showed me three newsletters from missionaries her church supports and added, "They're a little preachy." She was right! When missionaries don't take time to select a ministry story to write about, they often revert to teaching their latest devotional, which can sound preachy.

Sermons belong in the pulpit, not in your newsletter. Missionaries can "preach" when they view their newsletter as a forum to teach or preach biblical truth. Sharing an occasional lesson learned is okay, but a consistent diet of that is not. <u>A sermon is about "them," whereas a lesson learned is about you</u>. Keep it personal. The goal: use your newsletter as a way to communicate God's work in people's lives.

Sample 1 - PREACHING

Greetings from the Boston area with ten inches of snow. Grace to you and peace from God our Father and the Lord Jesus Christ. He has risen. Death is swallowed up in victory. Now thanks be to God who gives us the victory through our Lord Jesus Christ. The Passover was a fantastic night of deliverance but nothing like the turning away of God's wrath on the cross for His elect and the empty tomb of our Savior who is now sitting at the right hand of God!

Sample 1 - NOT PREACHING

Though shoveling ten *more* inches of snow in Boston, we are excited. A couple in Bible study with us, Pamela and Bryan, are going deeper with Christ and sharing their lives and the gospel with peers. Pamela said, "I was so scared to tell Katie about Christ, but she listened and is willing to read the Bible with me!"

Sample 2 - PREACHING

Our independence from God keeps us from obeying and trusting Him fully. We think, "I don't have time. I really don't want to do that."

However the Lord does not want us to live as if we did not need Him. He loves us! He knows everything about us, including our attitudes and actions when we are with other people and when we are by ourselves. God says that without faith it is impossible to please Him. So one question is, "Are we truly living by faith? Are we trusting God, especially in the 'hard' areas of our lives?"

One way to live by faith is to obey God even when it does not make sense, or when it is hard. Because when we obey, it reveals that we trust God and we trust His sovereignty. We trust that His ways are above our ways.

Sample 2 - NOT PREACHING

Jack asked me to do something I did not want to do.

Jack is a teacher at North Newton High School, and last month he asked me to talk to one of our basketball players, Derek, about showing up to practices on time. Derek had a bad attitude about a lot of things.

I prayed. Then I approached Derek. It turns out that Derek's mom was having trouble at work and was sometimes late in getting him to practices. I gave Derek a fellow player's phone number (Tony) to call if he needed a ride. Derek did call Tony, and they rode to practices together.

Tony then invited Derek to our Young Life Bible study and Derek came! Derek is new to the Bible and asked some questions like, "What is an Old Testament?"

God clearly reminded me of His lesson for me: Obey God even when it is hard or may not make sense. That shows that I love and trust Him. And look what God did in Derek's life.

9. Eliminate or explain the jargon.

"We're excited to lead a DFD study with the TMS for our 3-E ministry," makes perfect sense to me. But what about my readers?

Do not assume your readers know your in-house ministry and organizational terms. Either explain them or eliminate them.

JARGON	JARGON EXPLAINED
We're excited to teach a 3E seminar at the April 20 Catalyst Conference in Bloomington.	We're excited to teach an evangelism and discipleship seminar for student ministry leaders April 20 in Bloomington. It's called the Catalyst Conference.

 Check out the next newsletter you read. Circle the jargon you find. Look out for some of these words:

Examples of Christian and Organizational Jargon

heart language	quiet time	FTC
saved	STINT	PD
Wheel Illustration	change agent	witnessing
Four Spiritual Laws	MK	Bridge Illustration
DTS	scope	SIL
DFD	AOA	support staff
2:7 Series	BWC	LOA
man-to-man	testimony	TMS
FSKs	a Timothy	

10. Keep your newsletter length to one or two pages.

Why is it that one-page newsletters are inviting to read? I was taught that a one-pager is the best, assuming it is well-written. However, when including a photograph or two, prayer letters can stretch into two pages. In general, most letters beyond two pages long lose readers because all that text seems like blah, blah, blah.

Occasionally a four-page letter is effective. Example: a "trip report" from a two-week ministry trip to Brazil with eight pictures, lots of white space, and informative captions.

35 IDEAS FOR A NEWSLETTER TOPIC

EVANGELISM/OUTREACH
- Someone who became a Christian
- Someone in the process of coming to Christ
- Penetrating question your friend asked
- Discovery from surveys about student's spiritual interests

- Monthly discussion group
- Life issues Bible study

DISCIPLESHIP
- Profile of someone in your ministry. e.g. What is her life and culture like? Perception of God? Changes in walk with Christ?
- Significant lesson someone learned at Bible study
- Challenges faced. e.g. Incorporating Christian principles on the job, peer pressure, moral standards
- Important lesson learned about sharing one's faith
- Challenge in ministering to busy people
- Mentoring someone how to disciple another Christian
- How you help a new Christian grow
- Emphasis on missions/reaching the nations

EVENT
- Transition and/or move to a new ministry assignment
- Changed attitude or life during a conference or missions trip
- Accident that impacted you or another person
- Conference highlights and what God taught someone in your ministry
- Special event, like a spring break trip. One woman wrote a famous "chili" story from her trip that people remembered years later. She followed up by sending out the recipe.
- Work projects for outreach

OPPORTUNITY
- Important ministry decision and how you made it
- Special speaker or event (e.g. Evangelist coming to town)
- Outreach efforts to Olympic athletes
- Child evangelism studies during the summer

OBSTACLE
- Ministry obstacle you dread
- Visa situation
- Local authorities banned meetings in the dorm
- Hindrance to the gospel

TRAINING/DEVELOPMENT
- Important lesson learned
- First three steps when training a new staff
- The process of training up a leader for church planting (Idea: chronicle it.)
- A change in your thinking (Tell it through a vignette/story.)
- Impact of a literacy program on a student or parent

CULTURAL ISSUES
- Humorous or unusual custom
- Particular beliefs. e.g. Superstitions, rituals, festivals, traditions, work ethic, spiritual beliefs

Tip 2: BEGIN WITH A BANG

> One of cartoon character Dilbert's Laws of Work:
> *"Important letters that contain no errors will develop errors in the mail."*

You have four seconds to capture someone's attention in your newsletter. If not, you've lost them. That is what is taught for direct marketing newsletters (Jutkins 2003), and the same holds true for your letter.

Your newsletter competes with piles of mail screaming for attention, just like the stack of mail on your table. A 2000 Pitney Bowes and the Institute for the Future study revealed that the average worker receives 204 messages a day, including phone calls, e-mails, voice mails, letters in the mail, faxes, and pager calls.

Without a super introduction in your newsletter, people will merely glance at it. Your newsletter needs to stand out, to have some punch. Invest 15 minutes and create a terrific introduction. (Thank you Alvera Mickelson for the phrase, Begin With a Bang.) Also, don't assume people will remember your last letter. Repeat brief explanations when referring to something or someone mentioned in a previous letter.

A respected advertising copywriter, John Caples, wondered how *Reader's Digest* handled introductions for articles (Caples 1974). In one issue, John copied down the first sentence in each of 35 articles. He observed six capable methods for introductions:

- Quotation
- News (There is a new committee in Washington….)
- Preview (Port-au-Prince, capital of Haiti, is the busiest, noisiest, most colorful city in the Caribbean.)
- Story (Anecdote or narrative of some kind)
- The Shocker
- Interrupting Ideas

These proven methods offer insights for newsletters too.

SIX REMARKABLE ATTENTION-GRABBERS

Attention Grabber #1:   Use a Good Quote.

> *"I felt like I was talking to someone who had risen from the dead,"* Jean said after we left the hospital room.

U S F
University of South Florida

"YOU GUYS HAVE CHANGED MY LIFE!"

JUNE 2002

This has probably been one of the most exciting, exhausting, and challenging years of our lives. This past Fall and Spring semester Jamie and I, along with our teammates Jeff and Karen, have facilitated Bible discussions in Beta dorm at USF. We've seen several students come to Christ and watched some of these young believers grow in

---

"When I first met you, I wasn't sure what to think. It's hard for me to trust because we have not been able to trust very many people. But now I do and I thank you for coming!"

Eighteen year-old Natasha told me this during our last week in Pyatigorsk, Russia. A year ago, she opposed a friend who had expressed his faith in Jesus. But like many of the 70 students who participated in our English Camp this summer, Natasha changed.

"I Opened the Door!"

Dear Friend,

The day was Saturday, May 15. The setting was Nairita Airport, Japan. I struggled through customs with five pieces of luggage, and then I caught the first glimpse of my new friend, Yuko. Little did I know then, but God would work some amazing changes in her life.

We exchanged a hug, introductions, and then we were off on a four-hour journey to Shizuoka City. Our new apartment had five rooms (including bath!). Yuko and Mariko, my two roommates, welcomed me with open arms and as we got to know each other better over the following weeks, I had the feeling that I had "come home."

Attention Grabber #2:   Start with an Intriguing Fact.

One hundred boys and girls lined up for breakfast this morning because their parents welcomed a nourishing meal for their children. Seven year-old Isabella was especially excited, and she had a surprise.

At Adopt-A-Child in Guatemala, breakfast and a Bible story is our morning routine twice a week. Each child memorizes a verse, and Isabella had a compelling question.

Dear Friend,

It was the first time I hitch-hiked in Russia, and I learned a good lesson.

Here in Russia a convenient and relatively inexpensive form of transportation is called flagging a car, any car. Most Americans would call it hitch-hiking, but here it is just another means of getting from here to there when you are in a hurry. The main difference is you pay for it.

You may flag (a gesture using your hand) any car coming down the street. When a person stops, you say where you want to go and ask how much it will cost. Sometimes the driver charges nothing because it was on his way. That's how I met Sergei, who gave me my first ride for free! I later found out Sergei was no ordinary teacher.

Dear Friends,

"Do ghosts eat Big Macs? Chicken nuggets too?" "Why are the incense sticks stuck in fast food?" These questions are all part of celebrating "Ghost Month," the seventh month on the lunar calendar. While China and Taiwan follow the Western solar calendar system of twelve months and 365 days for daily life, most Chinese people still follow the lunar calendar for determining seasonal holidays.

The first day of "Ghost Month" is called "Opening of the Gates of Hades." It is believed that the gates of Hell are flung open on this day so the ghosts and spirits can "eat, drink, and be merry" in the land of the living. For the next 30 days, every time we go out into the streets of our city, we see tables set up covered with food, flowers and burning incense sticks. It is a depressing sight!

Attention Grabber #3:   Begin with the important moment or high action point of the story.

January 20, 2003

I almost died. It was 1:00 a.m., February 15, 1991 and I was aboard the USS Tarawa during the Persian Gulf War. A scud missile attack had just missed the ship.

Though that was 12 years ago, I think about it again as I talk with our friend Mike. He is a corporal in the Corps and only days away from shipping out to the same area. He is thinking about scud missiles too.

Eyes, legs and dirty faces

I blinked as I checked the translation of Luke 18 concerning the rich young ruler. When Jesus told him that he should sell all his possessions and come and follow him, the text says, 'His face turned dirty.' Certain that this must be an error, I asked Laban to explain these words to me. It was then that I learned that it meant 'he became sad'!

Recently I revised the second half of Luke, as well as Colossians in preparation for the consultant check. It struck me again that the Rendille way of expressing things is so fresh and often so different. When Jesus foretells his suffering and death, the disciples did not understand what he was saying, or 'they did not have the face of it'. When the Jewish leaders tried to trap Jesus, he was not caught out, for 'he saw their leg' (noticed their attempt to trap him.)

To understand the text of Colossians takes a lot of unravelling. Understanding the text is only the first part. The challenge is then to find the best way to express the meaning in Rendille. However this must not be 'church language". It must always address the truths of God's Word in such a way that the camel herder and the woman sitting in the shade of her house making sisal mats, can understand the Words of Life.

The list of virtues the believer is to pursue, as well as some of the things to avoid, are very difficult to translate. Concepts such as humility and pride are difficult. However, covetousness is not hard. It is expressed in Rendille as *indoderdeeraan* (literally long-long-eyedness). This describes the person who is never satisfied with their herd of goats and sheep, no matter how many he has. They are always looking longingly at the other persons herds, resulting in long-long-eyes!

March 2, 2003

I never knew it would have this much impact. How could understanding the Latin root of the word "obedient" change everything?

How would you feel if you sent a 25 year-old woman home without the on-going oxygen supply she would need to live the rest of her life?

Difficult realities like this are part of my everyday life ministering in the hospital in Ecuador with HCJB World Radio. I want to help people physically and point them to Christ whenever I can. This woman's family lived in a rural area. What a sacrifice they made to admit her to the hospital because here, you have to leave a deposit of $250 to be admitted. That would be the equivalent of $2,500 for an American since the average Ecuadorian makes a tenth of what Americans do!

No place for soothsayers

Dufaankhasso (her name means *Slaughter-a-camel-ox*, referring to an event at her birth) had just returned home from the church service. She met two *moro* (soothsayers) who were visiting each hut in the Rongummo clan village. "I have just walked back from Korr, come later."

After some time, the two men were back again. "We can foresee that terrible things are going to happen to the boys of this village. We have come to ward off this evil, so you can give us some money to do the ritual." "Thank you for coming here today. However, I must tell you that I have a wonderful Keeper and Protector. His name is Jesus. He has saved me from my sins, and he is completely able to keep me and my children from all evil."

I bolted out of bed when I heard the harrowing screech, crash, and thump.

At 4:42 am, I stared through our bedroom blinds and saw some brake lights. I heard a stuck car horn blaring. My heart racing, my first thought was, "Where are my daughters?" Then I accounted for them both.

Next I started to dial 911. My wife Sandy said she already saw the police on the scene. After a few minutes, we tried to go back to sleep. But I could not get it out of my mind. "Was this another Marine on his way to work? Did he survive? Did he know the Lord?" I had to know.

By chapter eight Sergei could stand it no longer. He started asking questions like, "Who is Jesus claiming to be?"

Two days a week, Sergei (not his real name) and I meet at my office after he ends work to study Russian. We use the book of Mark as I read aloud and he patiently listens and corrects me. Russian is hard. For three months we have only discussed my pronunciation and points of grammar. But now Sergei started asking questions about the meaning of what we were reading.

Attention Grabber #4: Use a Startling Statement or "Tickler."

Thirty-three large pizza boxes, bones from fourteen slabs of ribs, twenty two-liter soda bottles..... I often wonder what our garbage collectors think when they come to our house.

The above was the remains from our **"Ribs & Bibs"** night when a hoard of eighty-five men swooped in for dinner and to learn more from Rich and Christine Oswald about who they are as men.

Dave   Julie   Lori   Cathy

Dear Friends,

I didn't expect his answer. It caught me off guard, but he was right—so right.

Dear Friend,

I had wondered if the struggle was worth it.

We learned the language, adjusted to the climate and culture in order to minister to Indonesians.

Masha (not her real name) had tears in her eyes when she realized.

She came to our High School camp and learned for the first time that sex before marriage is sin. As an unwed teenage mother, Masha immediately stopped sleeping with her boyfriend. This was no easy task, especially when one of our counselors visited Masha at her home and learned that the boyfriend lives with Masha's family!

Praise God for camp. At Great Oaks, we are committed to girls like Masha. She has been invited to stay at the camp for three weeks of Bible study and character development. That is one step in the right direction for Masha to discover true freedom and life in Christ.

Attention Grabber #5:   Ask a Question.

 Moscow Report   July 10, 2001

"Do you have what it takes?" This is the essence of three questions asked of Dean during our trip to Moscow in May. The questions were asked by the interpreter and a Navy Captain as Dean participated in several Bible studies with men and their wives representing all branches of the Russian military.

Question: How do you work backwards?

#6. Start with 3.5 billion people of Asian descent worldwide. About three billion of these people are not yet in our Father's Family, that is one-half of the world's population.

#5. Then consider the 11.5 million people of Asian descent in the U.S.A. Approximately 10 million of them are not yet in our Father's Family.

How do you reach neighborhood youth?

… Love them

"I want to be like Tiger Woods," said Robert, a 9-year old neighbor we take to school daily.
"You do?"
"Yeah! I bought some clubs from a garage sale. I dug a few holes in my back yard, and I play all the time. Everybody makes fun of me, but I don't care. I want to be like Tiger Woods. I've never been to a real golf course. Could you take me golfing Mike?"

What is the fastest growing religion in America?

Tim was shocked at the statistic. As a ministry leader in our church, he challenged six of us gathered in his office at 6:30 a.m. to pray that our church would produce committed Christian disciples. A new seriousness branded our hearts since hearing that Islam is one of the fastest growing religions in the United States! Our focus was never more clear: To raise up more church leaders and evangelists like William.

Are you ready for 4-11?

Last week on April 11, over 50 Campus Crusade for Christ students at the Auraria campus linked arms with InterVarsity to ask the 40,000 students on that campus if they were ready to face tragedy and even death if it happened to them. One student said, "I don't like to think about death, and I'm not sure what will happen to me."

Attention Grabber #6:   Use a quiz.

1,724

This is: A) My cholesterol level.
B) The number of hours I've been on the telephone this year.
C) The number of miles I drove in Illinois and Indiana to encourage and help missionaries.

It was tiring and exciting to log 1,724 miles of interstate and back roads in Illinois and Indiana last month. One conversation in particular with Greg (a missionary) was surprising.

What do African people need the most?
- A) clothing
- B) food
- C) school books
- D) Christ

The people in Uganda have heard the gospel story:
- A) often
- B) never
- C) seldom

"First, you must realize that no reader is going to wait for you. As a writer you must play the aggressor. It's your responsibility to stop the reader in his fleeting search for something to capture his interest."

—Robert Walker, *Leads and Story Openings*

Should I begin with a Bible verse?

Readers skip verses at the beginning of letters because they don't know the context of why you use it. It also has the potential to preach rather than tell a story. Instead, put the verse in the body of your letter to help readers understand its context.

Should I start with a greeting paragraph?

Greeting paragraphs read something like: "Greetings from Denver. We praise the Lord and hope you know His incredible faithfulness. God is so good and we are rejoicing in Him. It has been colder than normal this winter and Alice and I have battled colds and a bout with the flu." Frankly, friends skip these greeting paragraphs. So delete it and write a super introduction instead.

SALUTATIONS IN NEWSLETTERS

Whether to include a salutation (The greeting line in a letter, like "Dear Mike") in your newsletter is not a common question, but it is a great question.

In newsletters using letter formats, salutations offer a familiar and personal lead, just as if someone wrote, "Dear Mike," (if that is your name). A few salutations work better than others. In addition, newsletters without salutations work superbly too, with one stipulation.

SALUTATION	EFFECT	INSTEAD, TRY
Dear Friends and Family,	Not bad, but the reader may feel like it is written to a group instead of just to him.	Dear Friend,
Dear _____,	The reader may view a fill-in-the-blank as an impersonal form letter.	Dear Friend,
Dear Fred,	Wonderful! Using someone's name is personal and inviting.	Dear Fred,
No Salutation	Works excellent if you begin with a great lead sentence to draw in your reader.	No Salutation

No salutation works well with an excellent lead sentence.

February 2, 2003

I could not forget Pam's bombshell comment.

Four months ago I met Pam at the gym. We hit it off right away since we were both new to the military, and to the treadmill! Our friendship grew, and then normally upbeat Pam surprised me and said, "I love my husband, but really I am so depressed I don't think I can make it anymore."

Tip 3: ADD A PICTURE AND A CAPTION

Printed in a church bulletin:
"The peacemaking meeting scheduled for today has been cancelled due to a conflict."

A picture is still worth a thousand words. It creates a powerful visual link. It engages. One of my favorite newsletters features stories and pictures of friends from a ministry in Kenya. Their faces stick in my mind and connect me with this fascinating culture and God's amazing work there.

Corporate trainer Dave Meier with *The Center for Accelerated Learning* in Wisconsin compiled results from a sampling of nearly 2,000 training professionals of all levels and from all types of businesses. He found that 39 percent of these adults use visual cues in their type of learning (Meier 2003). Visual cues such as pictures dramatically enhance communication, learning, and appeal.

Adding a picture to your newsletter takes extra effort, but it is worth it! Think ahead a little. Especially captivating is a picture relating to your main story.

> "Keep in mind that some readers will not read your letter at all—but they will look at a picture and read the caption below it."
>
> —Scott Morton, *Funding Your Ministry*

TIPS ON PICTURES

1. Always include a caption.

Write a descriptive, sentence caption beneath your picture. Eyes automatically look at the picture first, then the caption. Captions get read, add flavor, capture details, and entice readers to read more of the letter. When writing a caption, express more than simply what the photograph shows. For example, for the picture below, instead of writing the caption, "Don, Mary and Joab," write:

At 7:30 PM each Wednesday, Don, Mary, and Joab study Ephesians with me and other singles who enjoy sharing Christ at their jobs.

Position captions for ease of reading. Directly below the picture works best.

I helped teach these enthusiastic Russian students English, and we studied some Scriptures about "Who is Jesus the Messiah?"

2. Use pictures that show action.

Action shots tell stories, and photos can convey feelings better than words. Use photos to capture the essence of a moment, not merely to record the event. For example, here is a group of students learning English. One of these pictures is more powerful than the other.

A good picture of Russian students learning English.

A better picture of some of the same Russian students learning English, in action.

3. Take pictures close up.

Do your readers need a magnifying glass to recognize anyone in your photograph? When taking pictures, don't worry about showing the background of your setting as much as getting a good close-up of people. Enlarging pictures tends to reduce sharpness, so move closer when taking pictures to minimize the need for enlarging.

Good picture, but distracting with the background.

I cropped this picture on the scanner to focus on the people and action.

4. Scan the picture into your computer.

Scanners allow you to scan photographs with high resolution onto your hard drive. You crop it while scanning. Digital cameras also take excellent pictures, show the image immediately, and can be downloaded directly onto your hard drive for printing.

5. Take lots of pictures to increase the chances of getting one good picture.

In general, it's good to ask ahead of time if you can take pictures at a ministry event such as Bible study or a meeting. People will get used to you taking pictures.

6. Use a picture with a clear image.

Gone are the days of grainy pictures in newsletters. Clear, crisp pictures communicate quality. In your original photograph, are the blacks black and the whites white? If you have a color photograph, use the one with the greatest contrast. Photocopy it to get an idea of what you'll end up with on your newsletter.

7. Keep film and camera on hand.

Ever had to run to Walmart for film just before Bible study starts? Do you keep forgetting your camera? If so, one idea is to keep a disposable camera in your briefcase. Or put the camera next to your wallet or purse so you'll remember to take it. Plan ahead by keeping a list on a 3x5 card of people/action photographs you want.

8. Include yourself periodically in the photo.

Friends like to see you in your picture. Ask someone else to take several shots with you in it. Ask people in your ministry to be the photographer at ministry events and activities. Coach them to get close and include you in the shot.

9. Make picture borders complementary.

With picture borders, simplicity reigns. The picture should stand out, not the frame. You can copy what is in style from other newsletters and mainline magazines. For example: A box frame around a picture was popular years ago, but not now. Though computers make adding graphic highlights easy, too many creates a "busy" look and your readers miss the content.

10. Use these four printing tips for pictures.

- <u>Pictures reproduce better on white (or light colored) paper</u> than on paper with darker or bold colors. White paper tends to strengthen the highlights.

- <u>Do not use preprinted photos</u>, such as those from newspapers or magazines. They reproduce poorly. Some may also have a copyright, including pictures from the internet.

- <u>Size your picture big enough to see.</u> Too small of a picture is just as bad as an unclear one. Do not make your reader squint to decipher who is in the photograph. Eliminate tiny pictures of an inch or less. Do not clutter your letter with dozens of small pictures just because you can. Make them easy for your reader to see.

- <u>Position the photo in your letter so that after folding, the crease of the fold does not go right across the faces in the picture.</u> This just happened in our last letter. Before you print quantities of your newsletter, print one copy, fold it, and check where the creases fall.

Tip 4: CHOOSE ONE THEME

Printed in a church bulletin:
"A bean supper will be held on Tuesday evening in the church hall. Music will follow."

In *Bored Readers Don't Pray Much*, Carrie Sydnor Coffman writes:

"A prayer-letter (newsletter) is an advertisement. You are advertising a ministry worthy of prayer and financial support. And 'the most important element of an advertisement is the idea,' declared my advertising professor at the University of Missouri School of Journalism."

"The problem with most missionaries' prayer-letters is the attempt to share an abundance of data. They try to tell about four couples in their ministry…or 23 converts…or everything they have done in the last three months…or all the highlights of the last year as many Christmas letters set out to do. **As a result, there is not sufficient space to include enough interesting details about anything to capture the reader's interest."**

"So he forgets all of it."

Carrie is right. Too much data repels readers.

Instead of clogging your letter with everything you have done the past four months, choose one theme for your newsletter. A theme frames your information and fosters retention. It gives ample space to expose depth of a story or an issue.

Here are excellent examples of one-theme newsletters.

"Your readers will understand you and your ministry better if you develop one topic well rather than floating around 16 topics of great interest only to you."

—Scott Morton, *Funding Your Ministry*

THE NAVIGATORS

*To know Christ
and to make Him known.*

July 1999

Dear Friends,

"Swan sensei[1], I'm worried about my health. I'm getting older, and I don't want to die as a Buddhist. Could I please attend your meetings to learn how to become a Christian? I've tried going to church, but it just doesn't fit me." That is what Arikawa shachou[2] said on the phone a few months ago.

My response was that I would be glad to read the Bible with her and help her become a Christian but that she didn't have to attend meetings. I said to her, "Let me read the Bible with you at your offices and include your staff, too." I've met with her and some of the office staff three times since then. What fun!

A few days ago, I was talking to another acquaintance, Saga Takuma. The conversation turned to purpose in life and what we want to teach our children. I was telling him that the purpose of the Swan family was to serve and love others because this is what Jesus taught. He answered, "I don't have a purpose. I know my purpose shouldn't be just to work. I know it isn't to make money. I know it isn't even to have and raise children. But I don't know what it should be. I haven't read the Bible and learned about Jesus yet, so how can I know?"

Saga san[3] is like a Japanese Cornelius (see Acts 10)—noble, open and honest of heart. We had already begun reading the Bible when the above conversation took place. I assured him that I would continue to read with him so he could learn about Jesus.

Pray for these two people that they would come to faith and that through them many of their associates and friends would also become followers of Christ.

These are two of the people with whom I'm currently relating and reading the Scriptures. This is what I live for—what fulfills me. The Lord has promised to make me effective in Japan as I share the Gospel: "I will make you into a threshing sledge, new, sharp, and having teeth. You shall thresh the mountains and crush them and make the hills like chaff." He has promised to train me in crushing obstacles to the Gospel in people's minds.

Now Jane and I are seeing another promise come true: "I will rejoice in doing them good and will assuredly plant them in this land with all my heart and soul" (Jeremiah 32:41). God is planting us by leading us into building a log house—an attractive place to live and minister for the next several years.

---

[1] Sensei means "teacher" in Japanese.
[2] Shachou means "company president" in Japanese.
[3] San means "Mister."

Campus Crusade for Christ

Sent to Siberia!!!

9 June 2003

Russia:

» only 10% of Russia's teens are considered "healthy"

» Tuberculosis is raging in Russia

» Russia has about 4 million heroin addicts

» Alcoholism, drug abuse & the use of abortion as the primary method of birth control have left more than 20% of Russian couples infertile

Eastern Siberia:

» covers 5 time zones

» Mongolia to the south, the Artic Circle to the north, the Pacific Ocean to the west, the rest of the world to the east

» severe winters & pleasant summers with more than 300 sunny days a year

Eastern Siberians:

» 450,000 un-reached students on more than 30+ Campuses

» 80,000 students in Irkutsk

» 14 un-reached people groups

» shaminism, animism & occultism are practiced by university students

» 1 campus team each in Irkutsk, Ulan Ude & Vladivostock

» 2 of our campus teams are multinational: American, Russian, Tatar & Korean

****

What's next:

-I will be at our national staff conference in Colorado from 13-24 July

-apart from that I will be raising the additional support I need to serve in Russia from about 7 June until early fall.

-I would love to be in Irkutsk before the snow falls

How the Lord has directed:

No, I have not done anything wrong! *Just moments ago* God has answered my prayer asking Him to send to Siberia.

For the last 9 years I have been asking the Lord if He would have me return to Russia to serve Him there. Over the years it seemed that His answer was, "wait" and even though it was difficult, I knew I needed to wait on His timing.

Just this last February I received an e-mail from the team in Irkutsk, asking me to consider joining them to help equip them to reach all students in eastern Siberia. The area is immense and the number of full-time missionaries in that remote part of the world are few.

Since I tend to be too quick to respond to needs, I took a few days to wait

to see if this was something I should seriously pray about. The very moment I began to ask God if He might be directing me toward Siberia, my mind was filled with ideas and plans and questions and more ideas about what we could do to make Christ known to a neglected and forgotten area of the

world.

I have been studying the lives of Moses and Joshua over the last year. The Lord used many passages in their stories to confirm to me that the time was now for me to return. He has continued to confirm His call through various people and situations.

Our region is everything to the north and east of Irkutsk, just to the left of Lake Baikal

What I will do in Siberia:

I was asked to join a "regional team" to lead and train the staff and students in that region in how to reach hundreds of thousands of people with just a handful of workers (exactly like what I am doing presently with the campuses in Colorado).

It is amazing to look back over the last 9 years to see

how the Lord has used this time to prepare me for the task ahead. I now have much experience "catalytic" or, apostolic ministry. My years in Colorado and now in Orlando coaching student leaders have given me much experience and "wisdom" in distance ministry. I am good at equipping and strategizing, and I love challenge and adven-

ture, so it seems that I am well-suited for this kind of opportunity. It also helps that I *love* cold weather!

I am so excited about what the Lord has in store for you and me as He moves us on to a new adventure in ministry. What an impact for Christ we can have on lost students in Siberia!

ONE story of helping a Christian disciple another Christian

Russia

SERVING THE NAVIGATORS IN RUSSIA

16 October 2000

Dear Friends,

Yesterday, while I was walking through the main building of the University, I bumped into Misha. His face was beaming. "Hey Dave, have you heard.?" My mind raced, wondering what I should have heard about. "Migal accepted Christ — he's now a member of God's family!" he said without hesitation.

Migal is a long-time friend of Misha's and when Misha's life began to change last year, Migal began to pound his friend with questions. Misha needed lots of coaching along the way as their discussions often ended in heated arguments. Misha liked to preach instead of share. He had forgotten the lengthy "process" that God had used to bring him to a personal faith. Over time, Misha began to see his friends world from his frame of reference and because of that, his life and words began to draw Migal closer to God instead of pushing him away.

Last week, on Thursday, I shared a simple illustration with Misha to help him see how he could share more directly with Migal. It seemed that now, six months later, Migal needed to be challenged with the "event" of becoming a Christian. Then, on Saturday, for four hours, Misha shared with Migal — there were lots of questions but in the end, Migal had to say that he was not yet a sincere believer. The "event" had not occurred — he had not "repented and believed." Less than a day later, Migal called Misha at 12:00 PM. "I need to talk with you Misha, can I come over?" was his request. Migal came and a couple hours later, he prayed to accept Christ into his life. The event occurred.

The process continues. Migal is already struggling — he's turned his back on the sin which was in his life, but the allure is still there. Now, my role is to help Misha mentor Migal as a new believer.

Misha saw God use his life to influence his best friend, Migal, to follow Christ.

This story is unique and special because Misha is the first young man from our ministry to directly influence another person to follow Christ. And this is why we are here. To see young Russian men and women influence others to follow Christ, to disciple them and to see them multiply their lives through friends and family. It is our hope and prayer that we can help give birth to a disciple-making movement in Russia.

On Monday evenings, I lead a men's Bible Study group of 12. Some of these men are staff, some are fairly new Christians, like Misha. Others have been around our ministry for 3-4 years. Our prayer is that each of these men would have a "Misha-like" experience and see God use their lives to lead others into a personal relationship with God through Christ.

You are an essential part of this work. Thank you so much for your prayers and gifts which allow us to be here. We thank God often for you.

SARS...and Salvation

June 2003

Has SARS affected Our Ministry?
So GLAD you asked!!!

If you watch the news at all, then you know about the panic over SARS, especially in Asia. It sent tens of millions of people into virtual hiding and cost billions of dollars in lost revenue to airlines, tourist sites, businesses and a host of other enterprises.

It emptied the streets of some of the world's most crowded cities, cancelled national holidays, and virtually closed down transportation hubs in major urban centers. It toppled powerful leaders, humiliated entire governments, revealed the inadequacies of an entire health care system.

It caused the cancellation of business meetings, conferences, vacations, and church gatherings. It has, in many ways, disrupted an entire culture, but as our director said, it has turned 1.3 billion peoples attention to the important things of life.

BUT, SARS has NOT stopped the Gospel of Jesus Christ from going forth in Mighty Power!!!

Here are just a few examples:

1) When the crisis reached one major city, a large group of foreign believers asked the local government if they could still have their weekly worship service. When no answer was forthcoming by Friday, the leaders decided to honor the "no answer" as a "no" to gather as a large group. As an alternative, they rented 20 large buses for the evening. As people came to attend the prayer service, they would load up a bus and send it out to circle the city with prayer. They ended up having 11 buses (about 525 people) traveling around that city—spaced out and going different directions—praying for about 2 hours each. It was a powerful time of lifting the city's leaders, people and sick before the Lord.

2) In one major city, the believers have felt a need to be proactive in showing the HOPE they have in Christ, in stark contrast to the hopelessness and fear they have been seeing all around them.

They have started a SARS Support Center in their local fellowship. They have packaged up medical supplies, along with a great book on hope in Christ and a brochure including a gospel presentation...and delivered thousands of these packages to people who are living or working in the local SARS hospitals and "Quarantine Centers".

In just the first week, over 3,000 decisions for Christ were recorded through these SARS Care Packages!

3) One of our leaders has received permission from the local mayor to set up a SARS Phone Counseling Center. People who are fearful, panicked, and hopeless can call in and get HOPE....in the form of a Gospel Presentation, along with sound counseling and encouragement. We are praying that this Center will be allowed to expand into a Nation-wide Center!

4) Many of our staff are reporting more spiritual fruit than ever before! Tens of thousands are turning to Christ because of the fear and panic that has been prevalent in the country. When they hear a message of hope, their hearts are naturally drawn to it.

Recruiting "Challenges"?

You would think that the SARS scare in China would make people give up on going there, even for the Kingdom's sake. Not so! *We have over 70 people processed and ready to go to China this summer....AND NOT ONE HAS BACKED OUT* as of this writing. That is truly a sign of God's call on these dear folks and of their deep desire and commitment to serve the Master!

I have really enjoyed doing the final interviews with these people. They are a good group. Thanks so much for your prayers for wisdom in processing their applications. Most of them will be going through cross cultural training starting the end of the month and then getting on a plane for China later in July.

Thanks for your prayers and support. He is faithful to provide through YOU!

In His love,

Connie

THE CASE FAMILY CHRONICLES

Serving with The Navigators at Cornell University

February 2003

Truth in the Inner Parts: On Asking the Eternal Questions

"Surely you desire truth in the inner parts; you teach me wisdom in the inmost place."
Psalm 51:6

There are many students who come to Cornell who have some sort of religious background. Chris is like that. He went to church when he was younger. By high school he had probably had enough of church. Chris ended up at Cornell and began to live the life of many freshman males: study hard all week, and then play hard all weekend long. Being a football player, Chris probably worked harder during the week than most freshmen and he definitely played and partied harder on the weekends. Even though initially Chris went the way of many freshmen, he hasn't continued in that path. You see, Chris's eyes were opened. By the end of the first semester, he began to see two things. He saw that the momentary pleasurable pursuits that consumed his weekends were not providing any meaning or purpose to his life. He began to view the life he was pursuing as unsatisfying, empty, even filled with futility in certain ways. Chris also saw something going on in the lives of some student friends of mine, something that was real, genuine, authentic, and hope-filled. He saw Jesus at work in their lives.

Here is an observation: The lives of 18, 19, 20 some things I see walking around campus are filled with distractions: lots of movies, music all the time, email several times a day, IM (instant messaging) through the wee hours of the morning. . . frenzied activity all the time. In some ways, you have to appreciate the sheer energy of it. But in most ways this energetic lifestyle seems almost designed to keep them distracted, to keep them from thinking deep thoughts about their lives and asking the really good questions, the eternal questions: "What sorts of things are really of value, lasting value?" "Where is real security found?" "Where do I go when I feel hopeless?" "What do I look to for real meaning in my life?" "What sorts of things are worth giving my life to?" The thing I appreciate about Chris is that in the midst of the chaos—which is the first year at Cornell—he stopped long enough to breathe, to consider the eternal questions. And I believe in merely asking those questions, he began to have big doubts about where his life was headed.

Last week, Chris prayed at the Monday night Bible study that Brett and I lead: "Thanks God for bringing me to these guys. Thanks for how I feel You strengthening me through Monday nights." God is surely at work in Chris's life. As exciting as that is, Chris is not the only guy that has stopped to breathe, to think about the eternal questions. Last semester, a football player named Shay stopped, asked the questions, and said: "I want to follow Jesus." This semester, Chris's roommate, Pat, is coming around, asking the really good questions. Tim's roommate Greg, is also asking about eternal things as well. Greg went to the Navigator Student Winter Conference and is pumped now about being a part of Monday nights. A guy named Tony has started to come around on Monday nights as well. Pray for these men. Pray that as God speaks to them through His word that they will make commitments to follow Christ and make Him LORD of their lives.

Chris

I have been praying Psalm 51:6 for all my student friends at Cornell, "Surely you desire truth in the inner parts; you teach me wisdom in the inmost place." I have been praying that as they ask the really good questions, the eternal questions that they would find their value, security, and meaning in God. That they would live for, care for and pursue the things that God cares about. That God would transform not only the things they think about, but also the things they care about.

Swanepoel Newsletter

A.I.M. International

THE RENDILLE HERALD

I am making a way in the desert—Isaiah 43:19

Second Edition, No 62 | **December 2002** | A.I.M. Int. PO Box 21010, Nairobi

Thank you for your vital role in reaching the Rendille for Christ. We deeply value all your love, letters, support, prayers and faithfulness. We could not have come this far without you.

We wish you a very blessed Christmas, filled with the joy & peace found only in Jesus.

Lord Alton comes to tea

To enter a Rendille hut, you have to turn sideways, and then squeeze hard. The entrance is very narrow. Ten of us packed into Dufaankhaso's little hut and sat on the cowskin 'bed' on the ground. It was a case of wall-to-wall fellowship. On the woman's side of the hut the fire glowed. Mugs of hot, sweet chai (tea, milk and lots of sugar all boiled up together) were passed around. This was followed by small square-shaped dough mandazis, and karanga (meat cut into little pieces and fried.) Lord Alton did not seem the least bit out of place – he seemed equally at home in Rendille country as he was when sipping a cuppa with colleagues in the House of Lords. As we slurped the steaming chai, Dufaankhaso told of her joy in knowing the Lord Jesus Christ. Others eagerly joined in. As we closed by singing, women and children crowded round the hut to hear what was going on.

David Alton and Mark Rowland had come to see the work amongst the Rendille. Mark works for Jubilee Action, a British Christian agency that sponsors the Loglogo Blind Project, that is run by the Tirrim committee of the Korr church. David is a founding member of Jubilee Campaign. David and Mark had just come from the Sudan where they had looked into child slavery. This is one of the many issues that Jubilee seeks to bring into the open. The next morning, we drove over the plains to Loglogo. The blind children sang, and displayed their skills at reading and writing Braille. David was given a tie of the Kenyan flag made of beads. He encouraged the children to persevere in the knowledge that learning provided opportunities that these children would never have had if they remained in their traditional lifestyle. The blind are a great burden in nomadic society and such children are frequently neglected and abused. However, this project is now making a big difference.

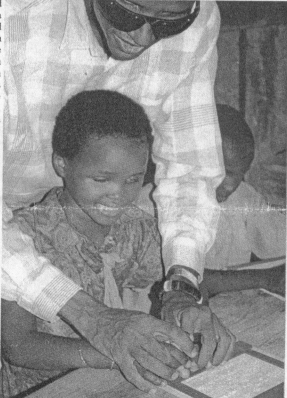

Osman, the blind teacher, skillfully guides a student in writing Braille

March 20, 2002

The countdown is on. The big event occurs May 2-6, in Minneapolis, MN. I'm referring to a four-day training for eight collegiate women who are a part of our pilot fundraising project, **"Breakthrough."** You may remember my writing about this project last summer. The training is the centerpiece of the project with preparation before the training and concentrated fundraising after the training.

Our Breakthrough design team, Glenn Balsis, Mike Gerhard and I have been steadily working on this for months. Here are just some of the factors we have been working through:

1. Inviting these women to participate and then waiting for their heart rates to slow down long enough for them to decided to let us help them with a scary endeavor
2. Communicating with each of the local supervisors to get their "buy-in"
3. Nailing down the dates and location for the training
4. Designing the curriculum – matching our three styles and opinions ☺
5. Ordering the supplies (this was the fun part – shopping!)
6. Hammering out a budget (this was not like shopping)
7. Lots and lots of emails

Actually, getting 15 people to find a common weekend for the training was like, well, getting 15 people to agree on the "best" color for new carpeting in a church foyer…many options, barriers, and finally compromises. But with the training date selected, the rest of the project is falling into place.

Preeeesenting...

Here are the women:
- Karma Bradley
- Mistie Hutchison
- Rosie Rodriguez
- Leihlyn Tinio
- Christy Haley
- Betsy Stiver
- Gretchen Becker
- Joanne Olson

Let me introduce **Joann Olson** from Eau Claire, WI. You met her in the last letter. She helped Glenn, Mike and I set the direction for this pilot by saying, *"Oh no"* or *"Well maybe"* or *"This is what would really help."* Joann ministers in her hometown of Eau Claire. I am delighted she is sticking with us

June 18, 2002

Dear Friends,

Thanks for praying for my trip to Eastern Europe last month! When I returned home, the following e-mail was waiting for me:

> Dear All,
>
> I'd like to thank you all for the involvement you had in arranging Don's visit at HIRO. As always, he had interesting and useful observations and gave me good ideas and advise. I have always something to learn from him, even if we just chat.
>
> I believe the fact that he is coming here regularly now is very useful and efficient because he gets to know the program better and is able to help in a better way.
>
> The only frustration I had was the poor job we did in organizing his visit and I'd like to thank him for being so flexible and understanding. I was also sorry that we couldn't spend more time together. We didn't have a clear agenda for the meeting but we accomplished a lot in the area of helping me enlarging my vision and discovering new areas to explore or think about.
>
> Next time, I'd like him to spend more time at HIRO, if possible. Thank you very much, Don and all who made this visit possible.
>
> Florica

Your prayers and financial gifts for our ministry are an investment in the lives of many Europeans like Florica! Thanks for helping!

In Christ,

⬤ THE NAVIGATORS

July 29, 2000

Dear Friend,

A cookie cutter or a combination lock? Each day when I drive through the north gate of the Air Force Academy, I have a choice. As I listen to cadets share their stories, I can respond with a "cookie cutter" approach, offering easy answers, pre-packaged plans, and quick-fix solutions. Or I can listen prayerfully, mentally "turning the dial of a combination lock", probing, asking questions, and waiting for the tumblers to fall into place.

One morning a cadet may greet me in the coffee shop elated because of a great test grade, or discouraged by an argument with a roommate. The next hour in the Academy library, another cadet may be disheartened by a pattern of defeat in his struggle with sin, or encouraged by high ratings in his military performance. One thing is certain: most will be exhausted as they face an avalanche of pressures. During each conversation, I pray for God's wisdom as the discussion turns one way, then another, and I wait for His Spirit to break hearts open to truth.

Here's a sampling of what I often hear:

- *Jim tells me he's been a master of deceit all his life. Although his dad's a pastor, Jim's found ways to fool everyone at home and at the Academy. Learning integrity will be an uphill battle. I share verses about the authority of the Word, but Jim fears giving over control of his life to God.*
- *Kory asks, "What do you do when you're trying to help three guys grow? I've got Manuel, Dave, and Matt meeting with me so they can be discipled, but I'm not exactly sure what to do!"*
- *Steve wonders how he can trust God—so many big decisions about his career path with the Air Force and the choice of a life partner.*
- *Paul wipes tears as he confesses how his rush of angry words may have discredited his Christian testimony in his squadron.*
- *Andy's convinced "learning to walk with God is so cool." But now he wonders, "What happens when I don't find His presence as real one day as I did the day before?"*

With each cadet, I slide a printed portion of a Bible passage across the table. "From this passage," I ask, "what can we learn about God's perspective on the issues you're facing?" I don't want to just "stamp out grass fires" week by week, but build lasting spiritual roots in the lives of each of these young cadets. I embrace the sentiment John expressed in 3 John 4: "I have no greater joy than to hear that my children are walking in the truth."

greetings from Steve and Mary

Serving with Wycliffe Bible Translators

January, 2003

FROM ORLANDO

Greetings from a chilly wet Florida!

New Years Eve NINE inches of rain flooded our street.

Here is the new Wycliffe clinic.

FROM THE PHILIPPINES

"Uncle, when will we translate some songs?" Dasul would ask each day.

Clay Johnston, our translator, was no musician. And, Dasul, with severe asthma and tuberculosis, was no singer. Finally, Clay picked some choruses. Together they toiled long, fitting in the patterns of Manobo. Verse after verse emerged. Eventually ten new songs told God's whole story from creation to resurrection.

Dasul's next request was even tougher. Clay must record these songs, so Dasul's family could learn them. Soon, Clay and Helen settled down each night to the sound of Clay's own voice wafting over the Manobo mountainside. The music caught on. Dasul's wife formed a ladies singing group. More songs emerged. Scripture and song was recorded and distributed together.

Today, Dasul is with the Lord. But the Manobo church, grown to 100 congregations and 7000 believers, is known as a singing church. Voices are commonly heard at dawn and bedtime. Children sing about the Lord through the day.

A man who could hardly breath helped touch an entire language group for the Lord through music.

Thanks to all of you who support us with your prayers and your generosity.

Steve, for Mary too

November 1999

Dear Friend,

It was a dramatic change! Tatiana's expression changed from one of worry to a full bright beaming smile that lit up her whole face.

She had just read the verse "I will never leave you nor forsake you!" (Hebrews 13:5b) It was evident that God had spoken to her so clearly by the change in her facial expression.

Tatiana's husband had left her and she was worried about how she would survive. Among other things she was afraid to be alone at night in an otherwise empty flat. This verse met both of her worries. How good of the Lord to encourage her in her need!

You may recall that I met Tatiana in the Canary Islands during Easter vacation last year. She lived across the street from me here in Pushkin but God led me 5000 miles in order to meet her.

She is now in Bible Study with Ira and myself. Ira leads the study. Please pray that she will continue to grow in her love for the Lord and His Word.

This incident reminds me of the Christmas story. Matthew 1:23 tells us that Mary's baby would be called Immanuel which means "God with us," one of my favorite names for our Lord. There is no closer relationship than the Lord living within us by His Holy Spirit.

During this holiday season, take some time out to review how God has been with you this year. It will do two things for you:

(1) It will give you a thankful spirit for celebrating the holidays.
(2) It will encourage you for the year 2000 to come.

Thank you for the way that you have been "with me" in prayer, love, friendship and support this year. May God richly reward you.

In Immanuel's Care,

ONE believer's challenge of living for Christ in the military

June 26, 2001

Cpl. Bryon Almeda at work.

Dear Friends,

Continuing with the series of *"A Believer's Struggle in the Marine Corps,"* We asked Bryon Almeda to write about Marines' profanity. He has been in the Marine Corps for two and a half years. He came to Christ in boot camp at a chapel service. His first duty station was at 29 Palms, Marine Base, where his life style was not much different from before, but he felt guilty. His second duty station was Okinawa, Japan where he connected with Cadence International ministry and grew in his walk with Christ. His third duty station is Camp Pendleton where he tied in with us eight months ago. He is now one of our key laborers for Camp Pendleton and lives with us.

Bryon wrote: *"Psalm 39:1 says, 'I will watch my ways and keep my tongue from sin: I will put a muzzle on my mouth as long as the wicked are present.' It's a challenge for me, but I wish I could sometimes take that muzzle and put it on the mouths of others. Have you ever spent a few weeks in the jungle as the only Christian among 50 marines, or spent two months in the desert as one of the three known Christians among 300 marines? I have, but it wasn't easy. Sure, I had a great opportunity to share Christ with others but what I had to hear from my marine buddies wasn't fun.*

Every day I'm faced with constant cursing, putting down of others, and degrading remarks about women. I have to stand in a formation to listen to my leaders use a foul mouth and harsh tongue to get their points across. I can't always just walk away from the bombardment of unedifying speech. To get away from it, I must seclude myself from others. However, the Marine Corps frowns upon that; they want me to work as a team. Instead I strive to set an example, speak wholesome talk, and edify words (Eph 4:29). However, after a while, their language begins to wear me down. It starts with coarse jokes and rude remarks, and before I know it, I'm laughing at the jokes or even standing in the circle with them. It's almost as if my ears get numb to their jargon. This is a perfect example of 1 Cor 15:33 - 'Bad company corrupts good character.' It's just so frustrating.

Another struggle is with those who disrespect God by using His name in vain. Daily I hear our Savior's name used as a cuss word. This is definitely the hardest as my ears will never go numb to that. It is also difficult for me to understand that right after some Marines bow their heads in prayer over a meal, one of the first words out of their mouths is very foul (James 3:9-10).

Sometimes, I can overcome the constant profanity by walking away and not listening. Mostly I have to trust God that He will let their words go in one ear and out the other. With His help, I know I can have the strength to walk away (Phil 4:13) and to keep a tight reign on my tongue (James 1:26). Please pray that my speech would remain edifying in the world where cursing, cussing, and using the Lord's Name in vain are accepted as the norm (Psalm 141:3)."

As you read Bryon's struggle, we trust this will help you pray for the people in the Armed Forces.

In Christ we labor,

40 One-Theme Newsletter Ideas

EVANGELISM
ONE person who came to Christ
ONE evangelism idea or event
ONE big ministry dream
ONE evangelism challenge
ONE ministry outreach started by someone in your ministry
ONE snapshot of welcoming cadets to the Academy and entering basic training
ONE way you used the Jesus film in your neighborhood
ONE way you use a team approach to reach your city for Christ
ONE person reading the Bible with you and a question she asked
ONE change or discovery in a person's attitude as he investigates Christ

DISCIPLESHIP
ONE Christian growing in Christ
ONE struggle in discipleship
ONE important ministry skill
ONE week of discipling four guys
ONE way God is using prayer
ONE leadership emphasis highlighting two couples with ministry leadership
ONE church and an example of how they apply discipleship
ONE focus on two women you are coaching to disciple other women
ONE way living as a servant is emphasized

EVENT
ONE overseas ministry trip
ONE significant celebration
ONE crazy month of May with weddings and graduations
ONE conference and one significant application from it
ONE spring break trip
ONE day of distributing Bibles

GROWTH
ONE impact of a mentor
ONE breakthrough in your ministry
ONE church that was planted and how it is growing
ONE seminar you taught and how it impacted a person
ONE need you face as ministry expands

CHALLENGE
ONE obstacle in ministry
ONE aspect of a foreign culture
ONE difficult aspect of military life
ONE aspect of what it takes for daily living in your culture (e.g. shopping for food, hand-washing laundry, dodging pot holes, riding your bicycle to work)

ONE way in how you decide which people group is next for linguistic work
ONE challenge on campus

OTHER
ONE part of training new staff
ONE transition to a new ministry emphasis
ONE aspect of your administrative job, like conference set-up
ONE part of training and encouraging fellow staff in raising support

When you feel compelled to cram a flood of information into your newsletter, the problem may be infrequent communication. Send a few more newsletters and you won't be tempted to squeeze in so much material.

Another gauge is to ask, "What would interest my readers?" Betty Barnett in *Friend Raising* tells of a missions' professor who assigned a survey of missionary prayer letters (Barnett 1991). "The result was shocking. His students discovered that most of the letters had little if anything to do with prayer, but were cosmic, super-spiritual expressions of God's blessing in a picture-perfect generalization, without any concrete description of what was happening in the field. Nothing tangible. Nothing to put a handle on in prayer." Guard against generalizations or long litanies of activities that often eclipse the main story. Give your readers something to remember and focus on a theme.

If you use a column format, it is more tempting to stray beyond one topic. Stick to a central theme for greater impact.

Tip 5: USE APPEALING GRAPHICS, DESIGN, AND LAYOUT

I endured a frustrating 30 minutes in Microsoft Word learning how to put a box around a logo. Another time I single-handedly wasted 20 minutes deciding which font to use.

Expect a few learning curves when working with design. However, if you spend more time on your graphics than on writing your newsletter, something is amiss. In *Editing Your Newsletter*, Mark Beach says it perfectly, "Design is important, but primarily to make content accessible. Without good content, design means little (Beach 1988)." Content is king. Emphasize great writing and let your graphics be simple and complementary.

Graphic design refers to how art, type, and other visual elements appear on your newsletter. It includes elements like: screen tints, lines and color, art, clip art, fonts, and pictures. The goal is to express, organize or enhance information to provide enjoyable reading. My purpose here is to give overall tips. Newsletter design books adequately address issues like designing templates and positioning blocks of information. Seek advice from a person skilled in design and graphics for your newsletter layout.

TIPS FOR GRAPHICS

1. Keep it professional.

Scott Morton in *Funding Your Ministry* sums it up, "You must use basic rules of design. Ask the unthinkable question: 'Can this be easily read by someone who is not in love with my software (Morton 1999)?'"

Steer clear of design clutter, smudgy copies, grammatical goofs, and typos. Correct spelling and neat design reinforce professionalism. Remember that your newsletter represents the organization with whom you serve. Pieces of art should not be a consistent substitute for photographs in your newsletter. Neither is adding a lot of bold, underline or italic highlights for effect a substitute for quality writing. Simplicity reigns.

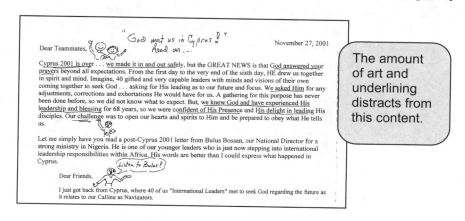

The amount of art and underlining distracts from this content.

2. Use clip art sparingly.

One newsletter cluttered with clip art made me not want to read it. Clip art was first developed for display advertising in newspapers, not for accompanying editorial matter in newsletters (Beach 1993). Though it can be used effectively, use clip art sparingly.

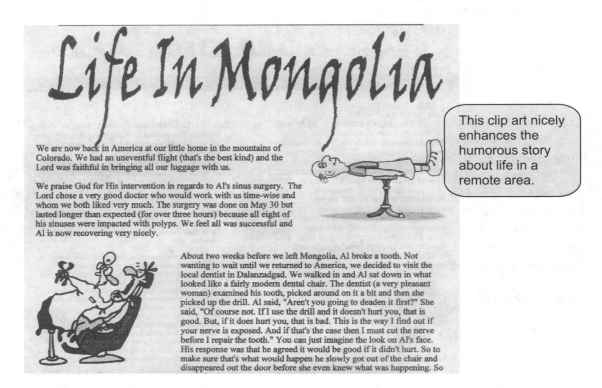

This clip art nicely enhances the humorous story about life in a remote area.

TIPS FOR DESIGN AND LAYOUT

1. **Choose a format.** There are two main formats:

   A. <u>Letter format</u>. This follows a traditional business letter format. There is a theme or purpose with an introduction, body, and conclusion. It lends itself to flow of thought around a central theme, while also giving flexibility for personal updates. This layout enhances a more personal feel as well. I much prefer it for these reasons.

   B. <u>Column format</u>. This is organized in columns or blocks of information. One consideration is that columns invite readers to skip around, like reading a newspaper. You may see no problem with that, but greater retention comes from a theme with flow of thought.

When designing your newsletter, solicit input from someone familiar with effective use of design—it makes the difference between people reading your letter or simply scanning it. In general, don't change the layout with each newsletter because layout consistency promotes reader recognition and familiarity.

Swanepoel Newsletter

A.I.M. International

THE RENDILLE HERALD

I am making a way in the desert—Isaiah 43:19

Second Edition, No 60 | May 2002 | A.I.M. Int. PO Box 21010, Nairobi

> Use an informative title to identify your newsletter.

Any colour, as long as its red

See overleaf

> Feature a theme, like this one on a craft course.

Desert happenings
—P 4

"Dogo mele"—P 4

Its coming!

The enthusiasm and excitement for the soon-to-begin building project is growing by the day. A deep thank-you from the Rendille believers for the generous help received to date. The fund is now at about 20% of the total costs. A German mission is currently drawing up plans for us and will advise us on technical matters. A local Somali trader has very kindly transported the first load of cement that we bought in Nairobi, without charge.

> Limit graphics and use lots of white space. A variety of graphic elements is easy to produce but can distract.

In the passage, women sit on the cement floor, hands flying as they fashion necklaces in intricate patterns. Over by the table, another group hardly looks up as they stitch handbags from dark blue denim. Not immediately visible, the men can be heard sawing behind the workshop area. One man is busy shaping a camel out of rock. The animal is crouched down on its haunches. Another files away at a miniature four-legged stool. In the main classroom, finished products lie untidily over the table. Wire 'trees' with red and yellow bead flowers. Pencil holders pressed from a mush of camel dung and newspaper. Painted shapes carved from stone combined with glass beads make an exotic necklace.

During the month of April, three young people from a church in Nairobi conducted a craft course in Korr. It was a stretching time for all. The young people found the draining heat hard to get used to. Plans to go jogging every day were quickly shelved. The course also was challenging to the Rendille. For a whole week, the necklace makers were denied red beads. According to the Rendille, there is no other worthwhile colour. Initially the men would not take part. Who has ever heard of stone being cut and shaped and filed? After a few days, the joy of discovery crowded out the other concerns. Blues and greens could indeed be used, even though red would have been best. Men sculpted rough rock into smooth treasures. Who could have believed that camel dung could be made into paper? Or that camel urine softened goat skins in the tanning process?

As fingers learnt new skills, and useless objects became valuable, joy and fellowship permeated the craft course. The Rendille women draped their sophisticated Kikuyu teachers in traditional goat skin skirts and ribirimmo, the bright head beads. Here was the heart of the matter. Not just products churned out on a production line, but people from different backgrounds becoming one. Precious friendships and prayer commitments are formed that strengthen the body of Christ.

The morning devotional time set the tone for the day. Those who were believers could be heard

New skills in the making

> Include sub-titles to make sections easier to read.

singing songs of praise as they worked. The final devotional was given to testimony time. Nariyo told of coming to Christ from her traditional setting. Having learnt to read in the literacy class, she avidly pores over the translated Scriptures. Now the Lord Jesus means all to her. Amina is one of our literacy teachers. She told of her conversion from Islam, and the great difference that Christ has made in her life.

The craft course is one of the ways in which we are trying to promote self-help for the Rendille. There are enormous challenges. Can we eventually bring the quality of the craftsmanship to a level where they can compete on the world market? Will we find buyers for these goods? With their normal confidence, the Rendille are puzzled by our hesitation. Of course it will sell!

2. Give plenty of white space.

Many missionaries cram something into every inch of space. However this gets in between the reader and your message. Don't be afraid of white space; it makes letters inviting, open, and easier to read. Aim for 20 percent or more white space in your letter.

- Use at least one-inch margins all around, and space between paragraphs, between columns, and around pictures.
- Keep paragraphs short—no bigger than from the tip of your thumb to the first knuckle.

Glance at the *design and layout* of the following six newsletters. Jot down how the layout makes some letters inviting to read and others harder to read.

_____

_____

_____

Spring 2002

News from Greg and Deb Snell

BROADER VIEWS:

Beyond Kitale

Dear Friends, we hope you will join us as we broaden our views to train even more of God's people in Africa and the Middle East!

Greg's Blessings

Our borders have expanded indeed! Over the next 10 weeks Deb and I will be staying in 17 different places in all, and experiencing what God is doing in West Africa. We start in Kinshasa, Congo where we will teach 100 WorldTeachers—men and women who will take this training to places we could never go. Then on to Yaounde, Cameroon to do more of the same, and hopefully see my old friend and classmate from Bethel Seminary days, Dr. Wilford Fon. Then on to Lagos, Nigeria and Accra, Ghana to visit ICM's work there.

Just today I read about a plane crashing on its way to Lagos and it reminded me of the temporal nature of our time on this earth. The odd thing is that the news of that crash did not cause me for a minute to reconsider this trip. Why? Am I just reckless? Do I not fear? I believe we all have mixed motives and at times know not our motives, but I do know at some level, that we go because God calls. And when God calls, planes still crash and people still die and protection from the fleeting moments of eternity must not ever dissuade us from our calls. Go in His peace.

What *is* That Beeping?

I had heard the alarm on Greg's watch several times that week. We were in the car one day and I finally said "what *is* that beeping for?" I looked at my own watch and said "what is happening at 3:30?" He said, "it's when I pray the Prayer of Jabez". Do you know that simple little prayer?

Oh, that You would bless me indeed,
and enlarge my territory,
that Your hand would be with me,
and that You would keep me from evil.

It's a short prayer in the Bible, tucked away in 1 Chronicles. Not without impact however! As we have discovered. Yes, we have been blessed. Yes, His hand is with us, and yes, He has kept us from evil, for which we are grateful. But it's the "enlarging our territory" that is the most dramatic! Since ICM forged a partnership with Walk Thru the Bible, our people all over Africa and here in the US have been praying that prayer, and God took it seriously! Phil Walker (ICM International Director) and Bruce Wilkinson (founder of Walk Thru the Bible and the author of The Prayer of Jabez) are in Nigeria as we write this, launching a new shared ministry called WorldTeach through ICM. In two weeks Ghana will also be opened. In June, our WorldTeach directors in Egypt will hold a launch for North Africa and 17 countries in the Middle East. When that launch is completed, ICM will have held trainings for 37 countries, along with ICM's formal and growing ministry in many of them.

The growth is no less than miraculous. Something is happening. God is on the move through ICM in Africa. These two visionaries, Phil Walker and Bruce Wilkinson, sharing common goals and dreams, are being used of God in amazing ways. At our staff meetings in California, we just shake our heads and say "how can common folks like us even dare ***dream*** something like this!" We say we couldn't have planned the movement of ICM the way it has unfolded over the last 18 months. Surely, God is directing our steps in His ministry.

And we are so blessed to be a part of it all. We are finding that our own personal territory has been expanded beyond Kenya and into all of Africa—our binoculars now take in a much broader view of God's plan for us, and we are ready to get in the boat, heading toward far more distant shores, toward people hungry for training to equip them for service in God's church.

Deb's Blessings

*It was so hard for me to leave Kenya. I didn't **want** my territory expanded! Enough, already! But guess what? I believe God knew I had dug my heels in, and He wanted to show me that He had more for me. But, I went "kicking and screaming" as they say. And now, a year later, I feel like the child who gets a shot and then through tears, smiles at the lollipop! And God is saying, "now, see, that wasn't so bad, was it?" I feel a new, expanded excitement about what He has in store for me. As Greg and I have watched and been part of the amazing expansion of ICM beyond Kitale, (just two years ago, Kitale and Uganda were it!) it's as though God is saying "did you think that was all there is?" He must love it when we receive His blessings and he hears us say, like children, "WOW!" Greg and I were saying the other day that we would like to do a study on Bible over and over to "be like little children". What joy there is in discovery! I discovered that when I can't be in Africa, Africa comes to me...we have had visitors come to California from Kenya, Uganda, Nigeria, Egypt—and I still have them in our home for ugali, matwakei and a cup of chai! God wants to use me and He wants me to go out with joy. May God enlarge your territory too!*

GUATEMALA

Mario, Paige and Jenni Miño

And Forbid Them Not

February 2002

It has been a privilege to serve both young and old here in Guatemala. However, the majority of the population that we minister to is very young.

Children can drain you of your time, energy and money. But that's OK because Jesus said, **"Suffer the little children to come unto me, and forbid them not: for of such is the Kingdom of God."**

Therefore, it is definitely a joy to serve the King by serving the owners of the His Kingdom. In the last few months, God has been impressing upon our hearts to impart vision into these young lives, particularly to the older ones. God wants them to know that they are important, that He loves them and has plan for them.

Rivers of Living Water

RIOS DE AGUA VIVA

We Painted a Sign for the Dueñas Church

Soccer has been a great way to form stronger relationships with all the children. The Guatemalans love soccer, but I believe that ***Mario*** is having more fun than anyone.

Another exciting development has been the beginning of a youth group. ***Jenni*** is especially enjoying meeting with the Guatemalan teens. Last Friday night we had 18 at our house. For many, this was the first time out of their small town of Dueñas. We are looking forward to many more fun hours of learning

Several of the 12-14 year olds do not attend school because they have chosen to work to help make ends meet in their homes. Please pray for these children.

GOD'S FUTURE LEADERS

Youth Group at Our House

Paige is excited about her new responsibilities as the Guatemalan AAC Coordinator in the Antigua Office. She is working mornings and continuing to study Spanish in the afternoons. The "señoritas" in the office are her special tutors.

LAS SEÑORITAS

Paige and the Adopt-A-Child Staff

Called to the kids.

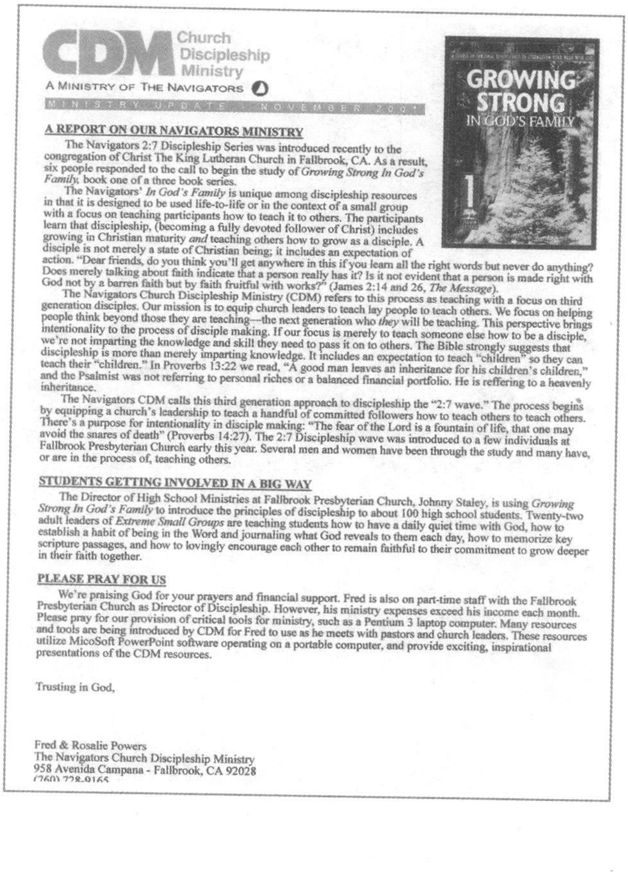

CDM Church Discipleship Ministry

A MINISTRY OF THE NAVIGATORS

MINISTRY UPDATE · NOVEMBER 2001

GROWING STRONG IN GOD'S FAMILY 1

A REPORT ON OUR NAVIGATORS MINISTRY

The Navigators 2:7 Discipleship Series was introduced recently to the congregation of Christ The King Lutheran Church in Fallbrook, CA. As a result, six people responded to the call to begin the study of *Growing Strong In God's Family,* book one of a three book series.

The Navigators' *In God's Family* is unique among discipleship resources in that it is designed to be used life-to-life or in the context of a small group with a focus on teaching participants how to teach it to others. The participants learn that discipleship, (becoming a fully devoted follower of Christ) includes growing in Christian maturity *and* teaching others how to grow as a disciple. A disciple is not merely a state of Christian being; it includes an expectation of action. "Dear friends, do you think you'll get anywhere in this if you learn all the right words but never do anything? Does merely talking about faith indicate that a person really has it? Is it not evident that a person is made right with God not by a barren faith but by faith fruitful with works?" (James 2:14 and 26, *The Message*).

The Navigators Church Discipleship Ministry (CDM) refers to this process as teaching with a focus on third generation disciples. Our mission is to equip church leaders to teach lay people to teach others. We focus on helping people think beyond those they are teaching—the next generation who *they* will be teaching. This perspective brings intentionality to the process of disciple making. If our focus is merely to teach someone else how to be a disciple, we're not imparting the knowledge and skill they need to pass it on to others. The Bible strongly suggests that discipleship is more than merely imparting knowledge. It includes an expectation to teach "children" so they can teach their "children." In Proverbs 13:22 we read, "A good man leaves an inheritance for his children's children," and the Psalmist was not referring to personal riches or a balanced financial portfolio. He is reffering to a heavenly inheritance.

The Navigators CDM calls this third generation approach to discipleship the "2:7 wave." The process begins by equipping a church's leadership to teach a handful of committed followers how to teach others to teach others. There's a purpose for intentionality in disciple making: "The fear of the Lord is a fountain of life, that one may avoid the snares of death" (Proverbs 14:27). The 2:7 Discipleship wave was introduced to a few individuals at Fallbrook Presbyterian Church early this year. Several men and women have been through the study and many have, or are in the process of, teaching others.

STUDENTS GETTING INVOLVED IN A BIG WAY

The Director of High School Ministries at Fallbrook Presbyterian Church, Johnny Staley, is using *Growing Strong In God's Family* to introduce the principles of discipleship to about 100 high school students. Twenty-two adult leaders of *Extreme Small Groups* are teaching students how to have a daily quiet time with God, how to establish a habit of being in the Word and journaling what God reveals to them each day, how to memorize key scripture passages, and how to lovingly encourage each other to remain faithful to their commitment to grow deeper in their faith together.

PLEASE PRAY FOR US

We're praising God for your prayers and financial support. Fred is also on part-time staff with the Fallbrook Presbyterian Church as Director of Discipleship. However, his ministry expenses exceed his income each month. Please pray for our provision of critical tools for ministry, such as a Pentium 3 laptop computer. Many resources and tools are being introduced by CDM for Fred to use as he meets with pastors and church leaders. These resources utilize MicoSoft PowerPoint software operating on a portable computer, and provide exciting, inspirational presentations of the CDM resources.

Trusting in God,

Fred & Rosalie Powers
The Navigators Church Discipleship Ministry
958 Avenida Campana - Fallbrook, CA 92028
(760) 728-9165

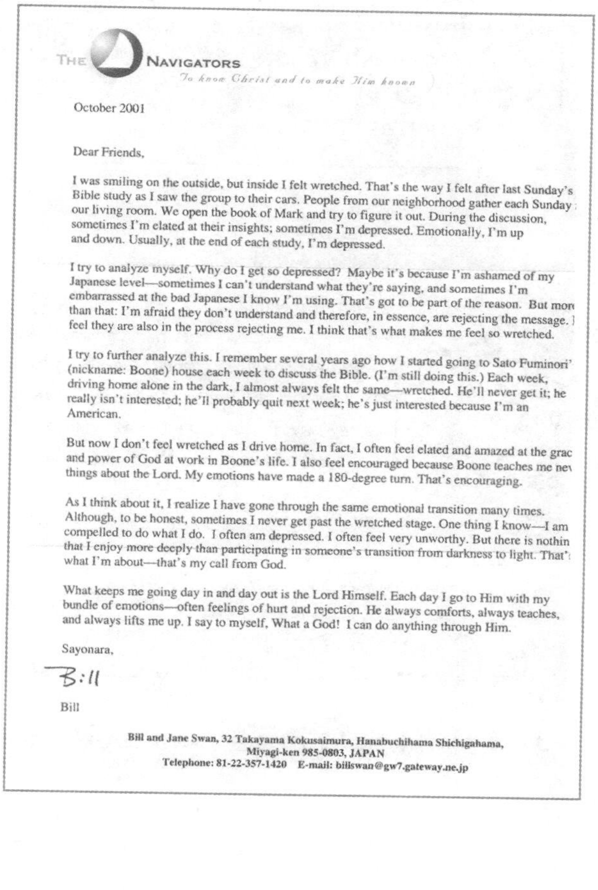

THE NAVIGATORS

To know Christ and to make Him known

October 2001

Dear Friends,

I was smiling on the outside, but inside I felt wretched. That's the way I felt after last Sunday's Bible study as I saw the group to their cars. People from our neighborhood gather each Sunday our living room. We open the book of Mark and try to figure it out. During the discussion, sometimes I'm elated at their insights; sometimes I'm depressed. Emotionally, I'm up and down. Usually, at the end of each study, I'm depressed.

I try to analyze myself. Why do I get so depressed? Maybe it's because I'm ashamed of my Japanese level—sometimes I can't understand what they're saying, and sometimes I'm embarrassed at the bad Japanese I know I'm using. That's got to be part of the reason. But more than that: I'm afraid they don't understand and therefore, in essence, are rejecting the message. I feel they are also in the process rejecting me. I think that's what makes me feel so wretched.

I try to further analyze this. I remember several years ago how I started going to Sato Fuminori' (nickname: Boone) house each week to discuss the Bible. (I'm still doing this.) Each week, driving home alone in the dark, I almost always felt the same—wretched. He'll never get it; he really isn't interested; he'll probably quit next week; he's just interested because I'm an American.

But now I don't feel wretched as I drive home. In fact, I often feel elated and amazed at the grac and power of God at work in Boone's life. I also feel encouraged because Boone teaches me ne\ things about the Lord. My emotions have made a 180-degree turn. That's encouraging.

As I think about it, I realize I have gone through the same emotional transition many times. Although, to be honest, sometimes I never get past the wretched stage. One thing I know—I am compelled to do what I do. I often am depressed. I often feel very unworthy. But there is nothin that I enjoy more deeply than participating in someone's transition from darkness to light. That' what I'm about—that's my call from God.

What keeps me going day in and day out is the Lord Himself. Each day I go to Him with my bundle of emotions—often feelings of hurt and rejection. He always comforts, always teaches, and always lifts me up. I say to myself, What a God! I can do anything through Him.

Sayonara,

Bill

Bill

Bill and Jane Swan, 32 Takayama Kokusaimura, Hanabuchihama Shichigahama, Miyagi-ken 985-0803, JAPAN
Telephone: 81-22-357-1420 E-mail: billswan@gw7.gateway.ne.jp

3. Choose a readable font.

Last week I struggled to read a prayer letter printed in a fancy font, and I quickly gave up. Well-documented research indicates certain typefaces (fonts) read better than others. People comprehend text in a simple serif type (with a serif) much more than in sans serif type (without a serif). Serifs are tiny lines that cross the ending strokes of most characters. They make reading efficient by helping the eye move easily along the line.

Here are a few widely accepted fonts for newsletters. Use no more than two different fonts in a newsletter. Points of interest and emphasis in your letter are created through changing the font size and weight, not by using different fonts (Beach 1988, 1993). The recognized standard font size for letters is 12 point. If tempted to print in a smaller size, you have too much material.

For Newsletter Text

Serif
(With tiny hooks on certain letters to guide the eye from letter to letter.)
Garamond
Palatino
Times Roman
Bookman
Souvenir

For Newsletter Headlines

Sans serif
(Without the little hooks on certain letters.)

Helvetica
Avant Gard
Arial
Futura

> **Avoid fonts like these that are snazzy but difficult to read.**

Dear Friends,

I seem destined to view beautiful mountainous terrains and sprawling Latin American cities through the small portal of an airplane window! This particular vista is where my heart still wants to call home. Bogota, Colombia. Where bombings, kidnappings and violent death are, as they say in these parts, "el pan de cada dia" (daily bread!). And yet, where also exist the memories of twelve years and the friendsphips of a lifetime. Sometimes I ask myself the question, "Really,

Note from the Editor: Our family is doing well. Jennifer (14) is playing soccer and loves school. Scott (18) is leading a Bible study, working as a tutor, giving guitar lessons and getting ready for college.

4. Avoid bright or dark-colored paper.

I cannot read Christmas letters printed on red or dark green paper. Literally. Text printed on bright or dark-colored paper distracts the reader, is difficult to read and causes friends to glance at your letter rather than read it.

<u>Paper colors that enhance readability include</u>: white, off-white, ivory, beige, and light gray (Rubin, 2003). These colors also convey a professional look. Light pastels work well too.

If you want bright paper because it reflects the age and persona of your ministry target—like neon orange for college students—that may work for a corporate newsletter or brochure, but not for your personal newsletter. Your eighteen to twenty-five year-old friends read your letters, but so do many who are older, more traditional, and less agreeable to reading letters on bold colors.

5. Use black ink to print your text.

All other colors like red, blue, green or brown ink are difficult to read. A very dark blue can work sometimes, but basically, stick with black ink.

6. Do not alter your organizational logo.

Have you ever seen an interesting adaptation of your organization's logo? Logos are usually copyrighted, which often restricts changes other than the size. Organizations may offer leeway for some variations of their logo, but not necessarily for your own rendition of it. Include your logo somewhere in your letter to signify you are not a lone ranger in ministry, but rather you serve with a reputable organization with accountability, vision, and leadership.

Tip 6: WRITE WITH VITALITY

You know you are stressed if you ask the drive-thru attendant if you can get your order to go.

Here is a "secret weapon" to transform mediocre newsletters into captivating ones and to boost your writing to the next level. First, think about a missionary letter you enjoy reading. Why do enjoy it?

Chances are it has some vitality! Vitality does not ooze from my pen. I rarely show my first draft of a newsletter to anyone because it stinks. That is because I bang out my thoughts and story without worrying about grammar, spelling or how it sounds. I write freely and I call it draft one. Afterwards, add vitality. Here's how.

Add Vitality (or Tabasco sauce) to a Newsletter

1. Edit, edit and edit your newsletter.

Exceptional newsletters require a couple of drafts at minimum. I edit mine three to five times. Write your letter then put it aside for several hours or a day or so to "cool off." Then return with fresh vigor. Don't be forced to think, create, edit and print within an hour. When I do that, I resent writing and my letter is boring.

Most of us use far more words than necessary. Effective newsletters are concise. Find a few words, phrases, or repeated text and delete or change them. Look for uses of helping verbs (is, was, are, were, to), and substitute with action verbs.

A MINISTRY STORY IN THE EDITING PROCESS

Draft One, unedited

Toru has been interested in lots of different religions and philosophies for a long time. He understands and knows a lot about Buddhism and how to live as a Buddhist. His is spending some time studying with a Shinto priest. As they were meeting and studying together for long hours, the priest got tired of it and said to Toru that he had the devil and wanted to not meet anymore nor continue with any relationship because Toru kept asking lots of questions that were hard to answer.

What to Edit

Toru has been interested in ~~lots of different~~ religions ~~and philosophies~~ for ~~a long time~~. He ~~understands and knows a lot about Buddhism and how to live as a Buddhist~~. He ~~is spending some time~~ studying with a Shinto priest. ~~As they were meeting and studying together for long hours~~, the priest ~~got tired of it~~ and said to Toru that he had the devil and ~~wanted to not meet anymore nor continue with any relationship~~ because Toru kept asking ~~lots of~~ questions ~~that were hard to answer~~.

Edited Version

Toru has been interested in various religions for 15 years. He is steeped in Buddhism and studied for four months under a Shinto priest. The priest finally lost patience, cut off the relationship and declared, "You are filled with the devil, " because Toru kept asking difficult questions.

> "Clutter is the disease of American writing."
> —William Zinsser, *On Writing Well*

2. Use action verbs.

In my favorite college class, Professor Brennan assigned a daily journal to record our observations and feelings from the numerous group activities she doled out. These activities pushed you out of your comfort zone.

Professor Brennan collected our journals, returned them, then announced that she saw a gaping hole—few students could communicate what they truly thought and felt! So she gave us one sheet of descriptive adjectives and verbs to help us be honest and communicate. It became a well-used resource! Following is a similar list of action verbs and words for vivid communication.

> "In general, you do better to transmit meaning through your verbs. Verbs shuttle the mind toward your goal."
>
> —Sue Nichols, *Words on Target*

Action Verbs and Words for Vivid Communication

abandon	chide	drift	freeze	lure	rally	stagger
advocate	choke	drop	frustrated	march	rattle	stammer
adapt	clamor	duck	fulfill	meander	refuse	steal
admit	clang	duel	fumble	menacing	reek	stimulate
add	clash	dump	gang up	mend	register	stoop
affirm	clutter	dupe	generate	nag	relinquish	stop
aim	coach	duplicate	gird	nudge	resist	stream
alarm	compound	dwell	glance	nurse	restrain	stretch
alert	compose	echo	govern	offend	ridicule	strive
amass	conclude	eliminate	grab	ooze	rifle	struggle
amuse	condemn	embrace	grasp	order	rip	stumble
angry	confiscate	employ	grin	oust	roam	succumb
animate	confuse	endorse	groan	overlook	roar	summon
arrest	conjure	endow	grunt	overwork	rob	swing
assume	conquer	enliven	hang	pall	round	tailor
attack	contend	ensnare	halt	panic	ruin	tangle
attract	convey	enter	heed	pant	rush	tap
avoid	convince	entice	hem, haw	parade	saturate	tear
baffle	copy	erupt	hesitate	pat	savor	threaten
balk	cover up	escape	hint	peck	seal	thrust
barging	cram	establish	holler	peek	scan	tighten
barricade	creep	evaluate	honor	peel	scatter	tire
beat	cripple	evoke	hover	perch	schmooze	toss
begrudge	curtail	examine	hurl	perk	scorn	tower
belt	cushion	exasperate	hustle	pick	scrape	trail
bewilder	cut	experiment	ignore	pierce	scrutinize	transform
bind	dam up	explode	illustrate	pity	sear	transmit
blend	dart	exploit	imitate	plague	shape	trip
blaze	dash	exude	impart	plod	shatter	trudge
blunder	debate	face	imply	pluck	shock	turn
blurt	deflate	fail	impose	pollute	shuttle	twist
blush	degrade	fashion	inhibit	ponder	sing	understate
boil	deliver	fear	infect	pore over	siphon	unload
bond	demand	feature	investigate	pour	sketch	vague
boost	denounce	fend off	jockey	promote	skim	venture
bobble	design	ferment	judge	prove	slant	vexed
bombard	detain	fidget	juggle	provoke	slice	vivid
boring	develop	figure	label	prune	smash	wade
bridge	devote	fix	labor	pull	smite	wallflower
bristle	devour	flavor	lack	pulse	snap	warn
build	dim	flee	laugh	purify	snatch	wave
bulge	ding	fling	launch	pursue	sour	weave
burn	dip	float	laugh	push	span	weep
burrow	disarm	flout	lean	quarrel	spend	winnow
cascade	discard	fly	leap	quibble	spill	wound
catapult	disturb	fog	lecture	quit	spot	wrap
catch	dive	force	limp	race	spruce up	wrench
center	doubled up	fork	loom	racket	squander	yell
chant	downplay	formulate		ransack	squeeze	zip

Newsletter paragraph	Add vitality and write in words from the "Action Verbs and Words" list.
Jake is not open to my efforts to develop a friendship with him. He does not share his true thoughts and he gets very angry at times. But then God allowed me to understand that Jake is very lonely and his unfriendly personality is just a cover-up for his intense loneliness.	Jake _____ my attempts at a friendship with him. He _____ his true thoughts and _____ in anger at times. But then God showed me that Jake's sour personality simply _____ his intense loneliness.

3. Give substance and accuracy to words denoting number, time and place.

NOT	BUT
many	600
few	four
a long time ago	twenty-five years ago
in the near future	in fourteen days
from one city to another	from _____ to _____
	(you fill in)

4. Use short paragraphs.

One newsletter with sprawling paragraphs seemed like a lecture where the teacher never paused to catch his breath. Another letter had a foreboding five-inch paragraph that looked like a glob of information!

Paragraphs require a single main idea with sentences that support it. When writing essays, longer paragraphs adeptly develop ideas. However newsletters are not essays. *Cliffs Quick Review* teaches that short paragraphs work well in reporting information without discussion (newspapers), dialogue, and in essays for dramatic effect or transition (Eggenschwiler 2001). Short paragraphs in newsletters read faster and draw people into your letter. General principle: Paragraphs should be no bigger than the tip of your thumb to its knuckle. Here is an example.

Which of the two letters below is more appealing to read?

Who would have guessed? For two months I have led a group of five students through a study on eternity with Christ and without Him. This resulted in part from my friend June telling me how her life has been changed by watching a play in Chicago featuring the question, "Why did you never tell me?" She was so deeply impacted by this question and the reality of a future home in heaven or in hell that she has been sharing with people everywhere. When June returned from Chicago she went directly to her sister and shared clearly with her. She in turn responded to the good news. This last weekend June worked at a hotel for the summer and spent most of the weekend sharing Jesus with Katie, one of the maids there. Katie put her faith in Jesus Christ. At this same time, June's cousin, whom June had led to Jesus, told her father about the gospel. He too put his trust in Christ!

Who would have guessed?

For two months I have led a group of five students through a study on eternity with Christ and without Him. This resulted in part from my friend June telling me how her life changed from watching a play in Chicago featuring the question, "Why did you never tell me?"

June was so deeply impacted by this question and the reality of a future home in heaven or in hell that she has been sharing with people everywhere. When June returned from Chicago she went directly to her sister and shared clearly with her. She in turn responded to the good news.

This last weekend June worked at a hotel for the summer and spent most of the weekend sharing Jesus with Katie, one of the maids there. Katie put her faith in Jesus Christ. At this same time, June's cousin, whom June had led to Jesus, told her father about the gospel. He too put his trust in Christ!

5. Write with a combination of long and short sentences.

It works. "Short sentences are the meat and bones of good writing. Intersperse short sentences throughout your writing for clarity and strength (Wienbroer, et al 2000)."

6. Illustrate.

Most missionaries miss this potent point. When you illustrate, people read your letter rather than scan it. Illustrate means *to show* rather than simply tell. It describes with pertinent detail and visuals and can involve the five senses (sight, hearing, touch, smell, and taste). It requires effort and editing because most of us do not naturally write this way. Be yourself. Include your humor, but work to illustrate. Here's how.

TELL (Not Illustrated)	SHOW (Illustrated)
I lead a weekly evangelistic Bible study at Dixon Paper Company. I'm committed to reach women in the marketplace, and God is doing some great things! These women are growing in their understanding of Christ.	It's 11:30 a.m., Tuesday, and I wonder what Tricia will ask today.
It's also exciting to encourage and equip these professional women to effectively multiply their lives as they come to know Christ and reach out to others.	I get a Wendy's grilled chicken sandwich and drive fifteen minutes to Dixon Paper Company. As I enter the office, I hear five phones ringing and one angry customer. Three tired-but-smiling women walk into the lunch room and we chit-chat for ten minutes.
	"We're on page ten," I remind them. Eyes dart down or away when I ask, "So, what do you think it means here when Jesus says, 'I am the truth?'"
	Silence. Then Tricia broke the quiet, "How can you know that He is right? I mean, why not follow your instincts?"
	It is exciting to reach women in the marketplace like Tricia with the gospel of Christ. I am also coaching Terrie (Tricia's friend and colleague) to lead an investigative Bible study like this next month at Dixon. Thank you for your partnership to help women find Christ and reach out to other women as well. Please pray for Tricia as she gets closer to trusting in Christ.

TELL
(not illustrated)

Peoria Area Youth for Christ partnered with four churches and led a large group of students on a mission trip to Mexico. We drove for almost two days in buses and vans. For many of these students, it was their first time out of the U.S. You should have been there!

Our team is laboring at a brand new camp facility along with two other work projects sponsored by the Baptist Church there. In the afternoons we are providing three different Bible schools for the local children.

Thanks for your prayers and finances. This trip is strategic to our Peoria ministry. As these students grow in their passion and willingness to live outside their comfort zones they become soul winners to reach out to their friends with Jesus' love.

Want to come too?

SHOW
(illustrated)

"I shared the Gospel with Maria and she became a Christian. That is the first time I have led someone to Christ!"

Holly told me that after our Peoria Area Youth for Christ mission trip to Mexico with thirty students. Four days on the road, with ninety percent humidity and ninety degree heat in Mexico City, and look what happened.

The Mexican Baptist Church provided a brand new camp facility alongside two other work projects. After three days, Holly and the others forgot about cell phones and shopping. She said, "I love God and I'm excited. I want these children to know Jesus!" Holly was able to lead 10 year-old Maria to Christ during camp. A week after returning home to Peoria, Holly also told me that she shared the Gospel with a friend in high school. Her friend accepted Christ!

Is it any wonder we are committed to these ministry trips, and to partnering with four local churches? Thanks for your prayers and finances that made it possible.

Each student "survived" with no air-conditioning and filtering their water. As of today, at least half of the students are eager to go again next summer. Want to come too?

Compare the impact of illustrating **ministry vision and strategy** in this example.

TELL – not illustrated:

Dear Friends,

It is exciting to see what God has done through target church planting in nations worldwide. Christ's Kingdom is growing!

Build My Church, a leading target church planting ministry which my wife Brenda and I had the privilege of helping in 1986, now proclaims, "Target church planting has caught on everywhere!" For instance, staff from *Build My Church* challenged the Ugandan believers to set high church planting goals. The reason: The evangelistic crusades the Ugandans held were well attended, but not as effective long term because churches were not planted. Today, the Christians in this important African nation have alone just completed planting 8,000 **new churches**!!!! Presently, as a result of this key organization's hard work, over 50 nations have already set future goals to plant three million new churches! Praise God!

SHOW – illustrated:

Dear Friends,

"We wanted to plant two new churches nearby and we are amazed at what God has done! God blessed us mightily."

Pastor Owinyo of Christ is King (CK) church in Uganda told me that last month. It was a great beginning! One thing I enjoy is training our church planting ministry teams worldwide to help native churches be more successful in evangelism and long-term discipleship. In 1986 my wife Brenda and I trained our *Build My Church* team in Uganda, who in turn trained church leaders at CK. Look what happened.

The challenge to CK: Set higher goals to plant churches in your area.
The reason: Evangelistic meetings alone are not resulting in new churches.
The result: CK actually planted *three* new churches last year, trained the church leaders in how to help someone grow as a new Christian, and the congregations are 30 new Christians and growing! Pastor Owinyo commented: "People are coming to Christ, but we needed help to organize and keep them growing in the Lord. Thank you for helping us."

In fact, Christ is King church is just the beginning. Christians all over Uganda have just completed planting 8,000 new churches! Because of the hard work of our *Build My Church* teams, 54 nations have already set future goals to plant over three million new churches! Please pray for these new churches to take root.

7. Do not complain or apologize.

You may feel guilty that you have not sent a newsletter in over ten months, so you begin your newsletter something like, "I'm sorry we have not written in a long time." But don't.

The guilt is your issue, not your readers. An apology draws unnecessary attention to your perceived negative or guilt. Your readers are not sitting around the kitchen table thinking, "It's been a long time since we have heard anything from Mike Missionary." Instead, realize that friends will be glad to hear from you, and launch into your letter with that in mind!

Watch out also for negative slants or complaining in your writing. It is unprofessional.

APOLOGIZING	NOT APOLOGIZING
As I sit down to write this, I realize many of you may have been wondering "What has happened to the Caldwells?" I am sorry we have not written sooner.	Since Bret came to live with us, things have been busy and overwhelming. Who knew that God was about to do something special? Our ministry here at the University of Georgia has grown these past few months. Carrie and I met Bret....

NEGATIVE SLANT	POSITIVE SLANT
We missionaries can sin so easily in our letters. We are sorry. We want to share what God has done. But it is so easy in our hearts to want you to think that we have been good missionaries, worthy of your support.	*"For 60 years I rejected God. I believed education was the answer to man's problems. But you have helped me see that God is the mastermind of all. I am simply amazed to know that He would love me after all these years."* John, a Stanford professor, told me this last week. We are thrilled and amazed and humbled. Here is how the Lord changed John's life.

8. Write in the active voice.

"The term 'voice' refers to the form of a verb indicating whether the subject performs an action (active voice) or receives the action (passive voice). Use the active voice frequently. It conveys more energy, and it results in more concise writing (Eggenschwiler 2001)."

In addition, "Active voice makes for forcible writing. This is true not only in narrative concerned principally with action, but in writing of any kind (Strunk 2000)." Spot the passive voice by finding uses of helping verbs (e.g. is, was, were, are).

PASSIVE VOICE (Receives action)	**ACTIVE VOICE** (Performs action)
The book was given to Tom by Bill.	Bill gave Tom the book.
There were a great number of dead leaves lying on the ground.	Dead leaves covered the ground.
The reason he left college was that his health became impaired.	Failing health compelled him to leave college.
My first visit to Boston will always be remembered by me.	I shall always remember my first visit to Boston.
The ball was smashed over the net by Al.	——————————————— (Put it in the active voice.)

NEWSLETTER IN PASSIVE VOICE

The reason eight Asian students gathered in our living room was for a World View Discussion. There were several students keenly listening as I taught my historical survey of ideas that have pushed God out of the modern worldview. The main reason that one young man felt depressed was that he feels forced by the world to march down what he calls a "road to nowhere." He sees the emptiness of life without God, but his main issue is that he doesn't feel much of a purpose in life.

NEWSLETTER IN ACTIVE VOICE

Eight Asian students gathered in our living room for a World View Discussion. Each student keenly listened as I taught my historical survey of ideas that have pushed God out of the modern worldview.

Ming (not his real name) felt depressed and told me, "I feel forced by the world to march down a 'road to nowhere.' I see life without God is empty, but I wonder, what is my purpose?"

9. If you don't like to write, find someone who can.

A friend or acquaintance in your ministry, church, or neighborhood is a good writer and may gladly donate his or her time to edit or craft your newsletter. Or hire someone to write your newsletter. This could be a tremendous boost to your communication goals.

Larry is a missionary who exuded spell-binding and humorous stories from his ministry. I leaned forward to hear every word. However, not so with his newsletters. They were surprisingly void of his tremendous stories. I later learned that Larry hated writing, and I concluded that Larry is a good candidate to hire someone to write his newsletter!

10. Use a metaphor.

What do the following two descriptions communicate?

1. Writing a newsletter is like Christmas shopping. I enjoy giving gifts to people, but I am glad when the shopping is over.
2. After I send out a newsletter with an exciting ministry story, it is like shooting a basketball and hearing the swish of the net.

Now you try it and fill in your response.
Writing a newsletter is like _____.

Last month I rediscovered metaphors and felt like a kid skipping around the playground. I attended a discipling seminar by Dr. Randy Raysbrook called, "Reaching a Person's Heart the Way Jesus Did (With Metaphors)." Enthralled, I realized it was like having a turbo engine instead of a four-cylinder for discipling, *and* that this applied to newsletters too! Here is what Dr. Raysbrook taught.

The American Heritage Dictionary defines a metaphor: A figure of speech in which a word or phrase that ordinarily designates one thing is used to designate another, thus making an implicit comparison, as in *"A sea of troubles"* or *"All the world's a stage."* (Shakespeare). The Lord Jesus used metaphors constantly. He knew that metaphors give instant meaning and many times you must engage the heart to get to the head. Here are a few examples:

Matthew 4:19	Fisher of men
Matthew 5:13, 14	Salt, Light
Matthew 7:24-27	Builder (house on rock)
Matthew 13:24-32	Farmer (good seed and weeds), Mustard seed.
Matthew 23:37	Hen gathering chicks

Consider the impact of these metaphors:
➤ Evangelism is like introducing someone to my best friend. Or,
➤ Evangelism is like pulling teeth.

➢ Reading the Bible is like having to do homework. Or,
➢ Reading the Bible is like listening to a favorite song that touches my soul.

To boost your newsletter, add a metaphor. It can be from you or someone in your ministry. Try it and fill in these sentences.

My Bible study is like _____.

If my Christian life were a thermostat it would be _____.

When someone prays for me, it is like _____.

Discipleship is like _____.

How to Create Metaphors for Your Discipling and Your Newsletters:

How is this ↓	Like this →	*Nature	Family	Agriculture	Art	Building
The Christian Life		Is a sunny day sometimes, a tornado other times	Is a party	Has seasons of plenty and seasons of drought.	Is like a finger painting	Some of us have weak foundations
Evangelism		.				
Creating Trust						
Create your own						

*The chart is from Dr. Randy Raysbrook, The Navigators. Other life areas to create metaphors from include: Sports, Medicine, Warfare, Industry, Body, Finance, Work, etc.

Tip 7: PERSONALIZE IT

An actual sign seen across the good ol' USA:
In the office of a loan company: *"Ask about our plans for owning your home."*

Yesterday the mail came and I immediately grabbed the personal letter, opened it, and read it. I love "real mail"—letters from friends written to me. For pen and ink, that is as personal as it gets!

Your readers love personal mail too, so the more you personalize your newsletter, the better chance they will read it. Here's how.

1. Write to one person.

If you begin writing your newsletter to all 425 friends on your mailing list, you'll quit writing. Instead, pick one friend or relative and write as if you were communicating only to her or him. I use my friend Laura, or my Uncle Bud, and automatically my tone becomes personal.

2. Use "you."

Only one person at a time can read your letter, so write like you are writing to one person. When editing, find phrases like "all of you," "some of you," "many of you," and change them to "you."

NOT PERSONAL	PERSONAL
Thanks to all of you for praying for us.	Thank you for praying for us.
Some of you may know we are moving.	You may know we are moving.

3. Include a specific date (month, day and year).

When you write a note to your grandmother, you include a date because it is a personal letter. Similar principle.

NOT PERSONAL	PERSONAL
Spring 2004	April 18, 2004

4. Sign each letter personally with an ink color other than black.

Today with high-tech everything, people notice! You can sign a stack of 500 letters in about an hour, which is less time than it takes to watch a favorite video. Although it may sound overwhelming, the investment is worth it! This is preferable over the increasing use of computer-generated signatures.

5. Include your first and last name and address.

I was surprised by what I saw. Posted on a bulletin board in the church foyer was my newsletter for everyone to see. It dawned on me that many people who looked at my letter do not know me, so I better include my first and last name on every newsletter! Also, friends have given my newsletter to their friends because of a relevant topic. Including my name identifies for them who wrote the newsletter.

6. Clarify who is writing the newsletter if you are a couple or have a joint newsletter with a friend.

This promotes a personal tone and is less confusing to your reader.

UNCLEAR AUTHOR

Dave and Jean are excited to minister to Asian students at….

Dave is….

Jean is….

CLEAR AUTHOR

My wife Jean and I are excited to minister to Asian students at….

I am….

Jean is…

7. Use a left-aligned margin, not a justified margin.

AVOID JUSTIFIED MARGINS
(blocked)

Do not justify the margins in your newsletter. That is for newspapers, not personal newsletters. Justified margins sap friendliness right out and create awkward spacing.

USE LEFT-ALIGNED MARGINS
(not blocked)

This left-aligned margin reads easy, like a letter. It uses a "ragged edge," which is more personal and less formal. Use it for your newsletter and your readers will appreciate it!

8. List prayer requests.

Friends want to know what to pray for, so give three or four prayer requests, but not a long "grocery list." Keep them simple but interesting. A few missionaries insert a bookmark-size prayer card with their newsletter. Your next letter or prayer card could explain how God answered those prayers.

Sample Prayer Card Ideas for your Newsletter
(print on cardstock)

Prayer requests for the Browns ministering at Purdue University

- That Brian, Kelsey, Scott, Lori, Bret, Justin and Michelle would come to Christ.

- For safety and character growth for ten students during our March 20-26 spring break trip to Tampa.

- That four students will sign up for a summer missions trip.

- For Greg as he leads a Bible study for young believers.

- For a good tutor for our son Joel in math.

- For Sandra as she prepares to speak at a women's conference.

Prayer items for Pete and Sarah Johnson, Spokane Community Ministry

➢ For co-workers to come and participate in our friend Stan's new investigative Bible study at his office.

➢ A profitable time for Pete as he attends a November 8-10 church leader's conference in Colorado.

➢ For God to bring Bruce, Angie, Kirk, Franz and Helen to faith in Christ.

➢ Isaiah 43:4 – ask God to give hundreds of people in exchange for our lives.

PRAISE:
➢ Sarah completed her counseling course.
➢ We got a replacement car for our Ford which had quit working.
➢ Bruce has been asking Pete about direction in life.

Tip 8: GET FEEDBACK

The Year's Best Headlines:
Kids Make Nutritious Snacks

Though it may intimidate you, ask for feedback on your letter. Feedback is an underused asset. When I asked my colleague Glenn for comments on my letter, he said, "This section sounds boastful." He was right! I also recently read a newsletter with two whole lines of text repeated. And I heard a damaging attitude from another missionary who said, "It doesn't matter what I write, I just need to keep sending something out."

No matter how quickly you want to "get this newsletter out," feedback will improve your letter. No matter how good you write, feedback will improve your letter. It goes beyond finding typos. A boring letter, grammatically correct, is still a boring letter! We make dozens of assumptions when writing, and it is impossible to catch them all ourselves.

Who can you ask for feedback on your newsletter?

- Friend from church
- Roommate
- Spouse
- Colleague
- Friend from Bible study
- College student
- Son or daughter
- Neighbor
- Donor

> ➢ Get feedback *before* you print your letter so you can edit and make changes.
> ➢ Give them specific ideas of what to look for when editing. Use the *Checklist for Editing and Proofing a Newsletter* on page 108 in the appendix.
> ➢ Give a deadline of when to get back to you.

Ask someone knowledgeable and willing to be honest. Let them speak to issues of clarity, flow, interest and pizzazz, as well as ferret out typographical errors.

I asked Kathy for feedback on my letter. She consistently said, "Your letter is fine." Although pleasant to hear, that was not much help! Later I learned Kathy hated writing and only aimed to be nice. I let her off the hook and eventually solicited feedback from someone else who gave constructive comments.

"Like apples of gold in settings of silver is a word spoken in right circumstances." Proverbs 25:11

PART II – ESSENTIALS FOR PRODUCING AND SENDING NEWSLETTERS

Has your enthusiasm for newsletters ever diminished because of the work required to send one out?

Oftentimes the hours required to print, fold, stuff, seal and stamp is as much work as writing the letter! Following are 16 questions with solutions to efficiently produce, mail out, and consider strategy issues for your next exceptional newsletter. Also discussed are ways to effectively use electronic mail (e-mail), and tips on sending newsletters when you live overseas.

Chapter Three – Production and Strategy Essentials

1. <u>How many people should I have on my mailing list?</u>

One missionary earnestly wants to pare down his mailing list of over 1,000 names. Why? High postage costs and the mammoth effort required to send his newsletter are a burden. Another young missionary racks his brain coming up with 50 names to begin his mailing list. Both of these men—though at opposite ends—wrestle with the same issue: How many people should I have on my mailing list? The answer stems from your underlying view of how to raise financial support for ministry, which varies from organization to organization.

An approach I have used with good success is a broad base approach. A broad base means build a big mailing list to include every Christian person you know, and then a hundred more! This is your constituency, the audience for your ministry. From that list, you hope to raise all of the financial support you need, both now and in the future. One rule of thumb: **For every $1000 in needed monthly support, there must be at least 100 names on your mailing list.**

When building your list, include people you consider acquaintances, even those you have only met once or twice. God may bring these new people into your life more to eventually support your ministry. I appealed to one couple I had never met before, and they have supported me for over ten years! God may also work things in people's lives as they get to know you and your ministry through your newsletters.

A. How do I get names for my mailing list?

One aspect of building a mailing list reminded me of the Israelites gathering manna for daily food (Exodus 16:14, 15, 31). God had *already provided* bread for them, but they had to go and get it. Similarly, God has called you to ministry and *already provided* people to support you and pray for you, but you may have to go and "get it." Start by building your mailing list.

Brainstorm through the categories listed below to jump-start your thinking. Do not worry about addresses yet; get them later. Think broadly. You know more people than you realize. Include past and present friends. Don't ask, "Who would support me?" Instead ask, **"Who would like to hear about what God is doing in this ministry?"**

As you brainstorm, avoid my mistake of "deciding for them." I would not add a person to my mailing list because of assumptions like, "They can't give because they have children in college (Fill in the blank.)." Do not exclude people; add them.

Areas to Brainstorm for Names to Build Your Mailing List:

- Work
- Churches
- Sunday School classes
- Bible studies
- Ministry teams
- School or college friends
- Acquaintances from back home
- Workout gym

- Sports activities or teams
- Hobbies/clubs
- Family
- Classes, seminars, conferences
- Acquaintances of friends
- Business contacts
- Professional associations
- Your children's friends and their families

Jot down names to add to your list:

_____

_____

_____

After adding a new name to your list (Becky for example), send Becky a copy of your most recent newsletter. Add a note like, "I mail out newsletters like this periodically and thought you might like a copy."

B. Should I have only donors on my mailing list to keep it manageable?

Pruning your mailing list to contain only donors is too narrow of a filter. Include non-donors on your mailing list to increase the potential pool of candidates for future fundraising efforts and prayer partners. Would you rather make funding appeals to people you don't know and who know little or nothing about you and your ministry? Or would you rather appeal financially to people who have followed your ministry and lives for a while through your letters?

C. What is the maximum size mailing list?

Many missionaries with budgets of $2,000 to $6,000 monthly (including all benefits, salary, taxes, ministry expenses, travel, and administration costs) have between 200 to 1,000 names on their personal mailing lists. There is no maximum size. One missionary caps his list at 150 names to keep it "manageable." However, he also remains consistently under-funded.

Keep a backup copy on disk of your whole mailing list, in addition to a printed copy and the one on your computer hard drive. Update the backup copy periodically. This protects you in case your computer crashes. If your computer crashes and you have no backup copy, you would have to hand enter all of the names again!

D. When should I remove names from my list?

Think again before removing names from your mailing list. One 15-year missionary colleague told me, "I am amazed by notes we receive saying, 'We pray for you every Thursday morning,' and it is from people I thought I should drop from our list!" Another Campus Crusade staff added, "One couple was on my mailing list for ten years and I had met them only once. Out of the blue, they started supporting me $100 per month!"

A basic rule of thumb: Do not remove names from your mailing list, even if you have not heard from them in years. Your well-written letter will minister to each person. God may surprise you. Circumstances change. Some people prefer occasional giving rather than monthly. Others love giving to one-time needs.

At the same time, a few missionaries with over 1,000 names on their list want to pare it down. If so, one way is to *pick 10 to 20 questionable names you may want to drop and send them a postcard they can return back to you.* Simply ask them if they would like to be removed from your mailing list, and make it easy for them to respond back—like a check box on your return postcard. Never send this postcard to your whole mailing list because that may inadvertently signal that your ministry stories are not worth reading.

Or, if you have over 1,000 names on your mailing list, you may have some people on your list whom you cannot remember who they are, or how you know them! You could delete these names.

E. Should I include non-Christian friends?

In general, have the majority of names be Christian friends and contacts, because they are the audience for your newsletters and the backbone of support and prayer. I send some non-Christian friends and family our newsletters for exposure to Christ and His Kingdom work. When I write the newsletter, this prods me to be sensitive to those who may be confused by a particular issue or story and to avoid jargon.

F. Should I include missionary peers?

It can be excellent professional development to include peers you work with—both current and past—on your mailing list. Peter, a Navigator ministry leader and friend, explains:

"I include peers on my mailing list. It is a professional courtesy to send my prayer letters to those I work closely with. I also ask to receive theirs. I am genuinely interested in their lives, plus this allows me to pray and learn from them too."

2. How often should I send a newsletter?

> Sign on a church door:
> *"This is the gate of heaven. Enter Ye all by this door. (This door is kept locked because of the draft. Please use side door.)"*

In an informal survey with 25 donors, friends, and missionaries, 48 percent voted to send a general newsletter three times a year, and 52 percent voted for four times a year. I recommend *a minimum of three times a year to your whole mailing list*; quarterly is even better! This is based on the understanding that you also communicate three to four more times just to your donors, who deserve more updates. <u>The overall goal</u>:

Donors hear from you: six to eight times a year (newsletters and donor letters)
Non-donors hear from you: three times a year minimum (newsletters)

Communicating more frequently to your donors allows you to focus on a topic in your newsletter rather than cram in a hurried recap of the last year's activities.

How Often to Send Newsletters: 3-3-1

➔ Send at least three general newsletters each year to everyone on your mailing list (donors and non-donors).

➔ Send at least three donor letters annually to just those who support your ministry. (A separate letter to donors only. Samples in the appendix.)

➔ Send one thank-you gift each year to donors.

Friends enjoy receiving your prayer letters, similar to the spirit of Proverbs 25:25: "Like cold water to a weary soul, so is good news from a distant land."

A. Send thank-you gifts.

Look for inexpensive items to mail to your donors each year. Gifts that connect with your ministry, cast vision, or remind donors to pray are powerful. Some examples:

- Campus logo key chain
- Russian calendar sketched by a friend in your ministry
- Nigerian toothbrush
- Military sticker
- Christmas ornament with a verse special to your ministry
- Cassette tape of a challenging message

- Book or booklet
- Bookmark distinctive to your ministry

3. <u>Should I write personal notes on each newsletter</u>?

A sign on a photographer's studio:
"OUT TO LUNCH: If not back by five, out for dinner also."

Who doesn't like personal notes? I read them first. I enjoy them. However, when writing notes on your newsletters, the huge amount of time it takes can cause you to avoid mailing out your newsletter, especially if you have several hundred names on your mailing list!

I asked a missionary, Mark, "What's the most difficult part of newsletters for you?" He answered, *"It's the pressure to write personal notes on most or all of the newsletters. We know people appreciate a personal word, but it takes a whole lot of time."*

It is a myth that a missionary should write personal notes on each and every newsletter. If your newsletter is well written, you do not have to write personal notes on all of them.

Instead of writing notes on all 500 newsletters, pick 20 to 40 and write notes on just those. Another idea is to rotate the group of names you choose for notes so that over a couple of years, each person will have received one hand-written note on your newsletter.

Another suggestion: compose one sentence and use it each time you write a note. That way you do not have to think of something unique for each note. For example: *"We appreciate you and pray you are doing well."*

4. <u>How do I avoid last-minute chaos</u>?

"Calendar, what calendar?"

I envy good planners. I can muster up an idea or two for the next newsletter, but it is a short list! Yet when I think ahead, it helps. It is not that hard.

<u>Jot down four ideas for your upcoming newsletters.</u>

	Newsletter Topic	Date to Send
1.		
2.		
3.		
4.		

A. Glean ideas from other missionary letters. Copy the good ideas.

B. Keep a brainstorming list in a useful place.

Add to it as ideas germinate. Pull it out when newsletter time comes and choose one. Ideas can originate from newspaper or magazine articles, an e-mail from a student, a memorable statement, a conversation, etc. One friend keeps his newsletter idea folder on his desk for quick access.

C. Mark it on your calendar.

Grab your calendar. Look three months ahead and pencil in a chunk of time where you can focus parts of your day on writing and mailing out your newsletter. Avoid the last minute chaos.

Sample Communication Calendar

	JAN	FEB	MAR	APRIL	MAY	JUNE	JULY	AUG	SEPT	OCT	NOV	DEC
Newsletter	✓				✓				✓			
Donor Letter*			*				*				*	
Thank-you Gift							●					
Prayer Team*												

* Sample donor letters are in the appendix.
** Numerous missionaries recruit committed prayer teams varying in size from two to fifty or more friends. They communicate regularly (e.g. monthly) with this team, often by e-mail. Letters in the mail can work well too.

D. Have a newsletter accountability partner.

Sometimes you may need a good "kick in the pants" to get out a newsletter. An idea: Ask a donor, praying friend, or fellow staff to be your accountability partner. This person has permission to hold your feet to the fire to get your letter out when you say you will. He or she can give encouragement, feedback and topic ideas.

E. Update mailing addresses every two weeks or monthly as changes and additions come.

Otherwise, it's crunch time to update addresses *and* produce your letter simultaneously.

F. Print envelopes ahead of time.

This idea is a winner! Print mailing addresses on your envelopes a few weeks ahead of when you write your newsletter. You can print them, or hire someone, or find a trusted volunteer to do the leg work. That way half the job is done when you are ready to print your letter! Plus it reduces excuses to not send out letters during busy times.

Also, consider buying pre-stamped envelopes with your pre-printed return address from the post office. It can save hours of time.

5. <u>Should I mention financial needs</u>?

> A shopping mall marquee read:
> *"Archery Tournament — Ears Pierced."*

Bruce and Amy have a dynamite ministry and have ministered in a few countries. They love people. They are servants. Their work is exciting and I love them. However, one day I stopped reading their newsletters.

For a while, every newsletter from them asked for money. I wondered, "Why are Bruce and Amy so desperate? Do they just want money from me?"

Low finances are stressful and can increase pressure to ask for funds each time you send out a newsletter. In times past I mentioned prayer for finances in my newsletter secretly hoping someone would take notice and give. However, low funding is often not the root problem. Hoping a newsletter will bring in all my needed income is the problem.

Consider another scenario. Suppose you sent four general newsletters last year, and in each one you included something like:

"Thank you for your prayers and support as we continue to raise finances. We are closer to our monthly goal. We only have $400 per month left to go and hope somehow it will be met."

"Please pray for our funding. It's been a rough few months with all of our medical bills."

"We're behind for the year in our support. We could use some extra income to finish out the year."

"We're doing okay but we're a little low in our support for two months. If you'd like to help out...."

From these four letters, what percentage of the time that your readers heard from you did you mention or ask for money? One hundred percent! A consistent pattern like that alienates people. As a general principle, do not use your newsletter as a vehicle to ask for money.

A. Is asking for prayer for finances the same as asking for money?

How you say it makes all the difference. Certainly ministry funding is a legitimate prayer request, but your readers may interpret a consistent financial prayer request as "hinting," or a "back-door," indirect appeal that is a veiled approach to asking for funds. Readers likely perceive, "Joe Missionary needs money *again*."

Instead, consider this missionary who gave an update on her funding. What do you notice about it?

> I have been incredibly blessed with very steady donor income…until this year. For the first time in over 14 years, I need to replace some support. I am looking forward to discovering whom God will lead to join my team to make up the difference in support.

B. What about providing "how-to-give" information in a newsletter?

More missionaries are printing "how-to-give" information in a side-bar or at the end of their letters. It sounds something like:

"All gifts should be designated for (name) and sent to (address). Please make your check payable to (organization)."

"Ministry support gifts as well as personal letters and gifts for (name) may be sent to (organization)."

When someone reads that in your newsletter, does it make him or her think about money? Could they interpret that as an indirect appeal? I think so. I do not recommend providing how-to-give information as a constant piece of your newsletter.

C. Is it effective to appeal for funds through a letter?

It depends. Keep in mind that letters asking for funds differ from a general newsletter and should state a clear purpose of asking for a financial gift.

For Monthly Support: Don, a friend of mine, sent 50 letters to friends asking them for monthly support. He heard back from only two people, so he assumed the rest did not want to give to his ministry. But that is a faulty assumption! I am positive many more of Don's 50 friends wanted to give, but life got busy and they forgot to respond or lost the letter. Instead of relying on a letter, consider that in general, fundraising for regular or monthly support works best when appealing in person, "face-to-face." In *Funding Your Ministry*, Scott Morton demonstrates why. He shows results from a study of 7,401 appeals from 100 Navigator staff (Morton 1999):

Appeal Method	Yes, monthly pledge
Face-to-Face	46%
Telephone/Letter	27%
Personal Letter	14%
Group Meeting	9%

For One-Time Ministry Projects: While raising personal support works best in person whenever possible, letters do have a place in raising funds. One excellent application is raising one-time gifts for specific ministry projects. Many Christians enjoy investing in timely and tangible ministry needs. Examples include:

- A conference
- Scholarships for camp
- Bibles to give away
- Missions trip
- Office equipment
- Moving to another country
- Timber to build a church in Nigeria
- Books and school supplies for a literacy class
- End-of-the-year appeal to "launch into next year"
- Overseas projects

<u>A financial appeal letter for a ministry project should include:</u>
- A tangible ministry project to fund.
- A sense of urgency (why you need the funds now).
- A clear purpose stated in the first or second paragraph. "I'm writing today to ask for your help with an important project."
- A clear "ask" for a financial gift. "Would you prayerfully consider giving $50, $100, $500, or $1,000 or more to help me get to Stavropol and reach Russian students for Christ?
- Instructions on how to give. "Please make your check payable to New Tribes Mission and mail it with the enclosed card by July 31."

In place of one newsletter, I sent an appeal letter to my whole mailing list asking for a special gift for an overseas missions trip. God blessed it and brought in all the funds!

Here is another good idea: When a donor increases their giving, even by $5 per month, let them know you are thankful! Acknowledge the increase and write a thank you to affirm them and their partnership.

6. <u>How can I segment my mailing list to manage communication issues</u>?

One of The Year's Best Headlines:
"Safety Experts Say School Bus Passengers Should Be Belted"

A colleague of mine said, "When I was a new missionary, I made a file folder for every donor and kept track of every communication with them…letters, thank-you notes, gifts, etc. It was fun! But that was when I had only 20 donors. Now we have 100 donors!"

How can you manage the mountain of communication issues? One solution: code segments of names from your mailing list. First, if you are just starting out, set up a database on your computer and type in all of your names, addresses and phone numbers. Have one field available for a custom code. Use various codes to keep track of communication and fundraising issues.

Sample categories for segmenting your mailing list:
- General newsletter
- Donor team
- Financial (with sub-categories such as: monthly donor, annual donor, one-time gift, not appealed to yet, funding appeal in person, and funding appeal by letter)
- Exempt
- Family
- Christmas card
- Prayer team

Try a few and see what works best for you. Keep it manageable and not overly detailed. Use a database that allows a place to type miscellaneous notes.

7. <u>What can I write about while serving in administration or leadership?</u>

> ➢ How I got lost on the first floor of the office.
> ➢ How I got lost on the second floor.

I served in support and leadership roles for 15 years and raised a portion of financial support. In picking topics for my newsletters, I considered parts of my job: answer phones, reply to e-mails, counsel people in raising support, create resources for staff, write and edit, set up and run conferences, and teach. This was exciting stuff to me, but captivating material for a newsletter?

Yes! Not because of the work alone, but because of the bottom line goal—changed lives. The same is true for you. Talking only about your work itself may bore readers, but here is the key.

Feature one part of your job responsibilities *and* link it to the bottom line of changing lives by including a ministry story or quote.

This bridges the fact that friends are not simply investing in your ministry to pay your salary, but to help change lives for Christ. Make it part of your ministry to illuminate why you are excited about serving in your role that is ultimately impacting people's lives. Here's how.

Describe one aspect of your administrative or leadership job:	**Link it to helping change lives:**
1. Secure a facility for a training conference.	1. "Our staff attending this training conference will get re-energized to return to the 'front lines' of ministry. Motivation will be stirred. Our staff will find new courage to help students like Josh, who recently found Christ through his college roommate."

2. Plan strategy for funding a new conference center for ministry growth.

2. "As I lead our team in deciding strategy for funding our conference center, the bottom line is exciting! We will be able to host more conferences, like our marriage retreats. At a retreat last month attended by 50 couples, one wife said, "If it were not for this weekend, I would have sought a divorce.""

3. Answer 70 calls and e-mails a day for your boss.

3. "Answering over 70 phone calls and e-mails daily for my boss Andrew may sound mundane, but it is exciting! One reason—it pumps my blood to see Andrew freed up to train our missionaries in various skills, like time management. For instance, one of our field missionaries, Ben, loves ministering to people. However, Ben spends more and more time at his computer and less time on campus with students. Andrew has been able to show Ben ways to be more efficient with his office work."

4. Overhaul an accounting procedure as the Chief Financial Officer.

4. "Today I celebrated as our team fixed a 'bug' in the missionary budget system that I oversee. Eliminating this bug saves each of our 1,254 missionaries over an hour this month as they process their new fiscal budgets. Setting a budget is not usually the most exciting task for a missionary, but now there is one less hassle. A wife told me, 'Thanks so much! I dreaded this budget process, but that worksheet is exactly what we needed and easy to use.'"

5. Shepherd a few of your 300 missionaries.

5. "Our three-week trip to Asia was tiring, but rewarding. Mary and I oversee ten missionaries in Asia. Cross-cultural ministries are challenging, and we are committed to take care of our staff in every aspect!

	Tom and Marge are one example. After learning they were exhausted, we helped set up a get-away so they could rest. Marge said, 'Thank you! I was so tired that I slept most of the first couple of days. It was exactly what Tom and I needed. Now we feel better, and we'll adjust our schedule so we can periodically rest.'"

Your role counts in missions work. Consider the baggage watchers in I Samuel 30:24. After the victory was won, some front line fighters complained and did not want to share the spoil with those who stayed behind to watch the baggage. But David declared, "…For as his share is who goes down to the battle, so shall his share be who stays by the baggage; they shall share alike." Similarly, you share in the victories of the missionaries you serve.

 Use a *word picture* in your newsletter to vividly communicate the importance of your role.

- Beth bounces around in her thoughts and ideas like a pin-ball machine. My desire is to help her center her decisions on the Word of God.
- Low funding for missionaries is like rust—slowly eating away. My job is to fix and prevent the rust.
- What I do is like working on NASA's mission control. Astronauts cannot get to the moon without mission control. Similarly, our missionaries cannot get to the mission field without essentials like visas and funding. I help them get both.

Chapter Four – Sending and Mailing Essentials

8. Should I mail my newsletter with first class postage?

> ➤ Pigeon mail is an option.
> ➤ Then again so is driving it there yourself.

Which mail do you read first—bulk rate or first class? Do you rip open the sweepstakes letter or the limited offer of 15 CDs and read it right away? Are you encouraged and inspired?

Your audience reacts much in the same way. With bulk mail, readers subconsciously categorize it as junk mail, something "not worth my time." I often don't open bulk mail.

Mail your personal newsletters first class. The extra postage is worth it! Long time fundraising trainers Scott Morton with The Navigators, and Betty Barnett with Youth With A Mission, agree you should send your newsletters first class. It communicates quality mail.

BULK RATE POSTAGE	FIRST CLASS POSTAGE
☐ Junk mail perception, toss it	☑ Quality perception, read it
☐ Arrives in 2-3 weeks (U.S.)	☑ Arrives in 1-5 days (U.S.)
☐ Stipulations on airmail	☑ No stipulations on airmail
☐ All exactly the same, no personal notes allowed	☑ Can personalize and individualize in any fashion
☐ Have to hand-sort and bundle	☑ No sorting
☐ Must have a paid permit to use	☑ No permit needed to mail
☑ Less postage expense	☐ More postage expense (but worth it)
☐ Minimum number required to send	☑ No minimum number of letters
☐ All letters must be mailed at the exact same time	☑ Can mail letters over a few day period, or anytime.

I stood in line at the post office with two trays of newsletters. After telling a curious man my letters were newsletters, he blurted out, "You should send those bulk rate…you'll save a lot of money." However he admitted it took him lots of time to sort bulk rate letters and prepare them to mail. He seemed impressed and amazed when I added, "We want our readers to perceive it as a quality piece and receive it quickly, so it goes first class."

Commemorative stamps are the best! They are fun and communicate a personal touch more than metered postage. Rolls of 100 self-stick stamps work fantastic. Metered postage can work too and sometimes save money if your non-profit uses pre-sorted first class. This stuffing and stamping routine is also a time where I pray over our newsletter and for friends on our mailing list.

For years I cringed at buying stamps for newsletters because funds were tight. I learned one helpful idea: create a budget for my quarterly newsletters including: stamps, printing, and envelopes. Incorporate that as part of the total funds I raise each year. When my support is raised, the financial pressure is off!

9. How can I get address updates quicker?

One of cartoon character Dilbert's Laws of Work:
"If it wasn't for the last minute, nothing would get done."

There are several endorsements you may include on your mailing envelope directly below your return address (U.S. Postal Office 2003). Each endorsement tells the Postal Service how to handle a letter if it cannot be delivered as addressed. Based on the endorsement, the letter will be forwarded to the addressee's new location, returned to you, or discarded. You pay additional charges for these services, and it can be an excellent way to get updated addresses. First-Class mail is forwarded or returned at no additional charge.

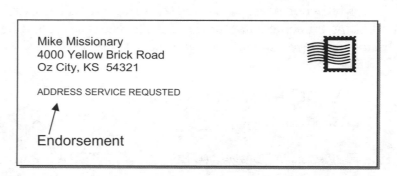

Here are the endorsements:

A. **Change Service Requested** tells the Postal Service to dispose of the undeliverable letter and inform you of your addressee's new location or why the letter can't be delivered. This service helps you eliminate inaccurate addresses from your address list.

B. **Forwarding Service Requested** tells the Postal Service to forward the letter to the addressee's new location or to return the letter to you if the recipient has not filed a change of address order in the last 12 months.

C. Return Service Requested tells the Postal Service to return the letter to you with the addressee's new location or the reason why it can't be delivered. This service is beneficial when you are sending valuable or personal items.

D. Address Service Requested tells the Postal Service to (1) Forward the letter to the recipient's new location, and (2) Return a copy of their new address to you when there is an address change of *less than one* year, or why the letter cannot be delivered. For address changes *over one* year, the letter will be returned to you if the recipient has not filed a change of address in the last 12 months. The current charge is seventy cents each. For each of our newsletter mailings, this address service costs approximately $25, and we save hours of time hunting down new addresses!

 After receiving an address correction, use that as an opportunity to express interest in your friend's life and send him or her a short note or postcard. Ask for an update on their life.

10.   <u>How can I save time and money</u>?

> ➤ Go to work for *Kinkos*.
> ➤ Live next to *Office Depot*.

- Print your newsletter in black and white instead of color.

- Keep your newsletter to one page.

- If printing on two sides and you want to include a color picture, limit the color printing to one side of a page, and print the second side in black and white.

- Invest in a quality, medium-priced color printer. Printing a color page yourself may be cheaper than paying a print shop like Kinkos. However it requires more of your time to print it yourself.

- **Pay to have your newsletter folded,** especially when mailing over 300 copies. Time is money. You can pay just $20 to fold 1,000 letters (.02 each) and you save a few hours of folding time! The idea is to let a machine save you valuable time.
    - o <u>Sign your letters after they are folded and have the letters folded so the area for your signature shows</u>. Provide a sample folded letter for the printer. This is my favorite option because we can sign our letters at home. It is also easy to add personal notes because no unfolding is required.

    - o <u>Sign your letters before they are folded</u>. After the print shop prints your newsletter, hand-sign all of them at the printers before they are folded. Wait there while they are immediately folded, then take them home.

- Pay a print shop to print your newsletter in black and white instead of running them off of your home printer. For over 500 two-sided copies, this can save you two to three hours of time.

- For newsletters with two pages, print your letter on one sheet of paper, front-to-back. Stapling two pages together is cumbersome. Also when mailing overseas, two pieces of paper can cost more in postage.

- Consider a postcard occasionally instead of a newsletter. This adds variety. However, do not routinely substitute postcards for newsletters simply to save money. Usually you cannot develop a story on a postcard, but you can give an update, or interesting event. Be aware that postcards may get lost or crunched in the mail more easily.

- Ask your photocopy location if they can give a discount or special pricing for your ministry. One missionary got a print shop to drop their price from eight cents to three and a half cents a page!

11. <u>What should I do if I have not sent a newsletter for ten months?</u>

> - Go to a ball game.
> - Wait until Christmas.

- Mail one out this month. Drop something from your schedule if necessary and make time.

- If money is an issue, talk to your ministry supervisor about financial help.

- Do not apologize in your letter for not writing sooner.

- Mark on your calendar to send out another one three or four months from now.

- Recruit a friend to help stamp and stuff your envelopes (to save time).

- Realize that if you don't write more frequently, you may lose a few donors. It will also be harder to get past the inertia after 11, 12 or 13 months of not sending one. Like the *Nike* commercial admonished, "Just do it."

12.   <u>What if I cannot afford to send a newsletter?</u>

> ➤ Eat Ramen noodles this week.
> ➤ Eat Ramen noodles next week.

- Ask your ministry supervisor for financial assistance.

- Pick three or four donors and ask for a special one-time gift of $50-100 so you can send out a letter next month. Include a deadline as to when you need the funds.

- Re-do your budget and include funds for a newsletter. Ask for help from your ministry supervisor if needed. In the next month or two, raise the needed support. It may only take two or three donors giving $50 a month to fund your newsletters!

- Ask your ministry team colleagues for some creative ideas.

- Consider a postcard update this time instead of an 8 ½ by 11 inch letter.

- Realize you will lose even more funding if you do not send out newsletters.

Chapter Five – E-mail and Personal Websites

13. How can I use e-mail effectively?

I have read dozens of e-mails from missionaries giving ministry news, updates and prayer requests. One rambles on and on. Another one forgot to add his name. Another preaches his sermon. Another sends her update as an attachment. Another one turns out to be a request for funds. However, some e-mail updates I eagerly anticipate. What makes them compelling?

The World Wide Web and electronic mail (e-mail) continue to revolutionize communication with faster modems, increased capabilities of sound and video, and faster downloading speeds. In this whirlwind, missionaries and missions organizations continue experimenting with effective uses of e-mail in communicating with their constituencies. For example, is it a good idea for a missionary to send general newsletters via e-mail?

I conducted an e-mail survey of 90 missionaries regarding their e-mail use with newsletters. The survey included new and veteran missionaries, ages approximately 25-60 years old (most were with The Navigators). Here are the results.

Missionary Survey—Sending Newsletters by Mail or E-Mail

- 81 percent send their general newsletter by the post office only.
- 14 percent send the *majority* of newsletters by the post office and only 1-50 newsletters by e-mail.
- 64 percent e-mail prayer requests and updates (different from a general newsletter) to select groups, including prayer teams and donors.
- 22 percent want to do more with e-mail.
- Three missionaries desire to get half or more of their newsletters out via e-mail, mainly to save time and money.

However, think before you e-mail. Sending more newsletters via e-mail entices because it is cheaper and faster. Yet faster and cheaper is not always best.

During my research, I heard a gamut of opinions on what makes an e-mail good or bad. There is also the issue of how often to send e-mails. The following are guidelines for using e-mail with newsletters. Keep in mind that *e-mail is a different communication medium than the printed newsletter.* Its style and messages are distinct. E-mails are more like phone messages, more "disposable" than printed letters. They can also be easier to "read later."

CAUTIONS WHEN USING E-MAIL

A. Keep it short.

A frequent complaint is that e-mails are too long. Most people do not like to read a lot on their computer screen because it is hard on the eyes, and who has the time? Today I received a missionary's e-mail newsletter. After a confusing introduction and scrolling past *ten* rambling paragraphs, I skipped it and hit delete. In general, e-mail is expected to be short. One effective approach: Keep your e-mail to a "screen full" so your reader does not have to scroll much. A rule of thumb: Keep it less than a page when printed out.

> "If an e-mail is not short, I won't read it."
> —Software consultant receiving 100 e-mails daily
>
> "If I can't figure out what an e-mail is about in the first few sentences, forget it."
> —Engineer

Do not assume friends will read your newsletters or updates sent via e-mail. One veteran missionary comments, "I am prone to read a printed newsletter even if it lays on my desk three to four days. But if it comes on e-mail, I'm in a hurry, will scan it then delete it. Don't assume people will read it just because it's easy to click and send to dozens of people."

Personal letters may be the exception. The Pew Research Center found in a May 2000 study that women, more than men, use the internet to rekindle relationships and track down lost friends and relatives. The study found that 71 percent of women, verses 61 percent of men, say e-mail has improved their ties with friends and family. That might explain why, in the last half-year, nine million women have gone online for the first time (*Say It with E-mail* 2000).

B. Do not send a newsletter as an attachment.

Very few people will take time to download and print your attached newsletter, except perhaps your mother. The more you ask your reader to do, often the less response there will be. If it has graphics or pictures, some computers bog down when downloading. My dial-up modem took four and a half minutes to download one newsletter with a picture. I won't do that again!

Many people use free e-mail services that do not support attachments or have trouble opening them. Some readers perceive that if the information is not important enough to include in the e-mail text, it is not worth reading.

For newsletters you want to send electronically, make them easy to open and read. Remove graphics and pictures. Shorten it and add subtitles. You might also add an introductory sentence such as, "Hello! We are sending our newsletter out electronically to a few friends who live overseas. Trust you are doing well, (your name)."

C. Recognize that e-mail is less personal.

E-mail is generic. You cannot use appealing formats, fonts or pictures with captions as easily. You cannot add personal notes to the receivers in a group e-mail. You cannot sign it personally. People do not often re-read e-mails, but they review printed letters.

D. Edit your e-mail.

Years ago when e-mail was new, few rules of writing existed. E-mails were meant to be created quickly, and writers often rambled, produced sloppy spelling and lacked development of thought. Henceforth, e-mail by its nature often fostered poor writing. This temptation remains.

Stop and read your e-mail before you send it to your prayer team. Edit it. Read it out loud. Use your spell-check. Write to compel interest.

E. Consider that you will miss part of your audience.

Be careful not to rely solely on e-mail as your main communication vehicle to your donors, non-donors and prayers. Also, don't substitute e-mail for things you can send in the mail. Consider these scenarios:

- Often, only one person at a time reads an e-mail, then deletes it. Husband Jim may receive your newsletter at his work e-mail. Chances are Jim may glance at it, but never print it out. His wife Renee will never see it, nor will his children.

- Vice President Bryan does not use a computer much. He will never even see your e-mail newsletter if it is e-mailed to his office.

- Not everyone uses e-mail. Several older people still do not have computers.

- Isabelle, a 24 year-old friend from church, has e-mail but prefers printed newsletters in the mailbox. She does not check her e-mail that often.

- Parents with teenage or college-age children may have a harder time getting computer time at home.

- One computer whiz who likes e-mail admitted, "There are ten to fifteen people who send me e-letters each month and I feel overwhelmed by them."

F. Consider the preference of traditional mail.

Here are some fascinating results from a Pitney Bowes household preference study in 2001:

> "The lure of electronic mail still draws headlines, but when the simple question is asked about mail preference, U.S. consumers still choose traditional mail. In March 1999, Pitney Bowes performed a mail preference study to address the growing emergence of e-mail in households, and in February 2001 the study was repeated. Not surprisingly, the main difference between the studies was the increase of households with access to e-mail from 34 percent in 1999 to 53 percent in 2001. What many may find surprising is the fact that *despite increased e-mail access, the preference for traditional mail remained virtually unchanged* (emphasis mine)."

People like paper mail. Another study conducted by Pitney Bowes and the ICR Research Group in 2000 revealed that *Americans maintained an emotional attachment towards physical mail* (emphasis mine). Surprisingly, a majority of people with access to e-mail kept mementos such as family photographs or birthday cards delivered by the postal system, while only a small fraction saved digital photos or e-mail letters. They also found that participants from all age groups remained committed to dependable, stalwart letter mail, particularly in light of the Internet's tendency towards viral attacks. In the categories of reliability and trustworthiness, *physical mail outranked e-mail by a margin of eight to one* (emphasis mine), and 66 percent of the participants preferred traditional mail over e-mail to securely deliver important personal and professional communication.

These preferences could be age-related since the younger generation has grown up with e-mail. The older generation is less prone to use a computer, is not exactly sure about e-mail and often prefers a hard copy of a letter. But for older or younger folks, I believe a paper newsletter has more "impact value"—interest, attractive layout, personable-ness, longer shelf life, graphic appeal, and can include a hand-written note.

G. Remember that e-mail is not secure.

E-mail is like a postcard—if you do not want it read openly, do not sent it. Your e-mail could also be forwarded by one of your readers to unintended receivers.

In addition, some ministry takes place in countries with restrictions or sensitive situations. If so, there are organizational confidentiality guidelines to follow.

H. Realize that some companies do not want employees to receive personal e-mail at work.

Companies pay their employees to do their jobs, not read personal e-mail. Even so, 85 percent of workers say they use company e-mail to send and receive personal messages (Fryer 1999).

Some friends may receive your ministry related e-mail at their work e-mail address. If so, consider the "business climate" of e-mails (DiSabatino 2001):

E-mail is not private in most businesses. E-mail received on company computers is considered company property. For example, "One company in the Boston area strictly enforces its policy of prohibiting employees from sending or receiving any personal e-mail." On the other hand, many small companies do not have any written polices for e-mail use, preferring to trust their employee's discretion. But a woman from one such small firm was asked if she thinks about what she writes before sending it. She said, "Sure, because anybody can read it. Anybody can go in the back room and pull it up on the server."

E-MAILS TO A PRAYER TEAM

A. Use e-mail to send prayer requests and updates to a group of friends.

I e-mailed ten friends asking for prayer for a weekend trip because we desperately wanted God to speak to the non-believers coming too. It lifted my spirit to know friends also pleaded with God for their souls. Afterwards, I e-mailed a two-paragraph summary of the trip and what God did.

Prayer is astounding. John 16:24 says, "…ask and you will receive, and your joy will be made full." Friends who pray undergird our ministry. Choose a few friends committed to pray and communicate with them. Remember that prayer requests and updates sent by e-mail augment, but do not replace, your newsletters.

E-mail prayer groups can include:

(1) Donors and/or
(2) Friends and family committed to pray but who may not give financially.

Build an E-mail Prayer Group

1. **Ask friends if they want to receive your prayer requests and updates via e-mail.** This invites them to be part of your prayer team. They can indicate where to receive your e-mails, at work or home. For example:

   "In a desire to partner with us in prayer, a number of friends have asked Cindy and I for some timely specifics regarding the ministry here at (your ministry target). So every two weeks or so I send out a short 'highlight/prayer' like the one attached. I don't want to fill up your e-mail box with information you won't read, but if you think this would be helpful for you, let me know and I'll send it to you. Thanks."

2. **Give friends an "out" if they desire to stop receiving your regular e-mail updates.** Include something at the bottom of your e-mail like:

"If you choose not to receive these monthly prayer e-mails, just reply and type 'unsubscribe' in your e-mail. There will be no hard feelings. I understand that you may receive excessive mail!"

B. Get ready to reply.

After sending out a newsletter or prayer requests via e-mail, be prepared to get some replies. Will you feel obligated to respond to ten replies? Can you make time to respond to them?

C. Use e-mail for an urgent prayer request, like an "SOS."

People often appreciate these specific e-mails. I valued one set of periodic e-mails regarding a friend's battle with cancer. It had answers to prayer too.

D. Do not write an essay.

Recently I received an e-mail prayer update that totaled a whopping 2,286 words! Having to page down several times created immediate disinterest.

TIPS FOR E-MAIL USE

A. Include a subject, salutation, and closing.

Type an informative subject line, salutation and closing in your e-mail prayer update. Include your name or ministry target in the subject line so people know immediately who it is from. Some examples:

E-Mail Subject Line (identifies the topic for your reader)
Camp Pendleton Prayer
Important Decision for Schneiders
Meyers Update
Italy Ministry Report
Hickham Prayer Items
UC Davis Prayer
Visa Needed for Sanchez
Urgent Prayer for Natasha

E-mail Salutation (helps personalize your message)
Dear Friends Who Pray,
Dear Prayer Team for (ministry target),
Dear (name),

> ## E-Mail Closing (helps personalize your message)
> Thanks for praying,
>   Coleen Williams (if that is your name)
>
> In His service,
>   Randy and Eileen Tuckerman (if that is your name)

B. Eliminate the huge list of names at the beginning of an e-mail by using Blind Carbon Copy (BCC).

Some e-mails (sent to a group) arrive with 50 or more names and addresses hogging the top of the e-mail. It is irritating to page down through these names to find the message. To avoid this, use the Blind Carbon Copy (BCC). It's a feature on your e-mail system. Go to the help button, type in "blind carbon copy" for instructions on how to use it. BCC allows each person to receive your e-mail without the other 49 names and addresses in the group who also received it. This also protects friends who may not want their e-mail address given out.

C. Use subtitles to make your letter flow smoothly.

Updates and ministry news are easier to read with subtitles, numbers, or bullets, especially in e-mails.

D. Choose how often to send e-mail updates.

What frequency works best for your ministry? It depends. Weekly updates are probably too often, for you and for your readers. Monthly or every other month may work well. Or consider an as-needed basis. Some missionaries send few if any e-mail updates.

Guidelines:
- E-mail updates supplement your newsletter, not replace it. Newsletters allow development of a newsletter story (with picture) whereas e-mails generally do not because they are expected to be brief.
- Regular e-mail communication is good, but can over-communication sour the receiver? I am reminded of Proverbs 25:17, "Let your foot rarely be in your neighbor's house, lest he become weary of you and hate you."

One missionary found that regular e-mails fortified his ministry while in Europe. Charles was sent from his church as a missionary to a sensitive country in Europe. While on furlough, a pastor of one of his supporting churches said, "You are one of the most prayed-for missionaries we have. You send your e-mails to get here in time for Sunday morning and we always mention what's going on in your ministry." Charles kept his e-mails short. He also noticed that some new support came from individuals and churches who had received his e-mails. Yet he also admitted his creativity dried up from a weekly demand to write, and he eventually stopped the weekly frequency.

E. Update and maintain e-mail addresses, including group lists.

When sending e-mails to a group of friends, create a group e-mail address list for your "send to" list. That way you avoid selecting each recipient's address every time you send an update. Instructions for group e-mails are available from your e-mail carrier. Go to the screen where you send e-mails. Use the help button and look under something like: E-mail – Sending to multiple recipients or group lists.

Regarding group e-mail lists, there is an extra step when updating addresses. After you update an individual address, go to the group list itself and update it there as well. Several carriers do not automatically update changes in group lists.

Unfortunately, e-mail addresses can also change quickly. Once an e-mail is returned "unable to send," there is no forwarding to a new e-mail address and no automatic way of getting the new address.

14.   Should I have a personal website?

> From the *Washington Post Style Invitational* contest of the worst analogies ever written in a high school essay:
> *"The little boat gently drifted across the pond exactly the way a bowling ball wouldn't."*

Personal websites are easier to develop and use, even for the non-technical person. This section does not teach how to develop and maintain a website. Rather it addresses factors to consider in having a personal website for ministry, or not.

Websites can adeptly profile you and your ministry, with your newsletter being one part of the profile. However websites are non-directed communication—people come to it. Regarding your newsletters, you want mainly directed communication—you go to people. You initiate and send your newsletters to people. Directed communication is the primary way to build your mailing list, and new contacts from your website supplement this.

Should I have a personal ministry website? Consider that websites:

- Give more information about you for those seeking it
- Offer resources (like Bible studies, articles, and links to related topics)
- Show a family portfolio
- Take time—to learn HTML language and keep items updated
- Provide fast updates
- Can offer an opportunity to invest financially
- Allow people to pick and choose what they want to read
- Can supplement your communication/fundraising mix
- Can serve donors/constituents who like to read and shop on the web
- Will continue to grow in use across all areas of life and business. One newsletter publisher said, "Forty percent of my income comes from companies that found my website."
- Supplement but do not substitute for personal ministry or personal fundraising

Chapter Six – Sending Newsletters While Living Overseas

15. <u>How do I send newsletters when I live outside of my home country</u>?

From the *Washington Post Style Invitational* contest of the worst analogies ever written in a high school essay:
"Her date was pleasant enough, but she knew that if her life was a movie this guy would be buried in the credits as something like 'Second Tall Man.'"

In *How to Write Missionary Letters*, Alvera Mickelsen explains, "Missionaries can exert influence on the perceptions of the Christian public and especially on pastors and mission-minded people in the local church. The letters you write may be the only contact your readers have with missions and missionaries."

"Your letters are the vital link between you and your readers, whether they are sent from the field or the furlough base. They affect the total missionary enterprise almost as much as the work you are doing on the mission field. Insofar as your letters multiply the number of new missionaries and stalwart prayer partners, they are as important as the meetings you conduct, the classes you teach and the witnessing you do."

Amen! It is invigorating to hear about God's work abroad. Friends will enjoy hearing from you when you live overseas. Guaranteed! Stay committed to well-written newsletters. Along with the ideas in this book, living in another country adds additional challenges with newsletters. A few countries considered hostile to Christians have a unique set of communication issues not addressed here. But for most countries, these ideas from seasoned missionaries help:

A. Recruit reliable friends in your home country to manage your newsletters in a professional way. Here are a few options:

- Choose dependable friends. Send them the content of your letter, including any photographs. Let them print it, stuff it, stamp it and mail it out for you. Make sure they have your addresses and address updates. It may be cheaper to mail your newsletters from the United States.

- Send your stuffed and sealed newsletters to a friend to stamp and mail from the U.S. This worked well for a missionary in Japan.

- Let friends manage your database of names (mailing list) for you. If your letters are sent from the U.S with a clear return address, you also might receive better address updates.

B. Pay a Christian newsletter service to manage your newsletters for you.

- Many large mission organizations have in-house capabilities to print and mail newsletters. Though it may not be the least expensive service, it could save you significant amounts of time.
  a) Set this up in advance. In addition to your letter and photograph(s), make sure they have:
     1) All of your updated addresses.
     2) A person (point of contact) to call if there is a problem.

  b) Expect a three to six week lag from the day you mail in your newsletter for printing to the day it arrives in people's mailboxes.

- Use a newsletter service. A few are listed in the appendix on page 124.

C. Consider mailing newsletters from your home country, if possible.

It is exciting to receive overseas mail with foreign postage! I loved opening the rice paper envelope from Taiwan missionaries. Using your host country's postage rates may be an affordable option.

D. Be aware that new frustrations may arise in sending newsletters while living abroad.

- You may not be able to write personal notes on any newsletters when living overseas. (Save those for your next home ministry assignment.)
- You may not be able to sign your newsletters personally.
- A few countries do not have quality copy services available.
- Some countries process mail quite slowly.

16. What if I am on home ministry assignment (furlough)?

> A sign seen across the good ol' USA:
> In the window of an Oregon store: *"Why go elsewhere and be cheated when you can come here?"*

Home ministry assignments are often packed fuller than expected. It can be hectic. Some may extend only a month, others a year. If your furlough is three months or more, this is a unique and potentially great time for writing a newsletter(s). You may be able to reflect on your missionary work with fresh insights.

Ideas to write about while on home ministry assignment:

- One of your furlough objectives and how are you accomplishing it, such as: travel, check in with your sending organization, visit people who support you, take a class, rest, visit family, study a certain topic, recharge spiritually, raise new financial support, renew friendships, recruit new missionaries for your country, go to a marriage conference, plan strategy for next year, or deal with a health issue
- A particular aspect of the culture where you serve
- A significant need in your host country
- An aspect that was hard to leave (in your ministry country) and why
- Reasons God tugs at your heart to return
- A spiritual or cultural belief held by friends in-country

Be sure you have your mailing list with you, a paper copy and on disk. This facilitates printing envelopes or labels for your newsletter stateside.

Example One - A Creative Furlough Newsletter

JOB DESCRIPTION	
Title:	Missionary on Furlough
Duties:	Visit people, travel, visit people, phone, recruit ministry partners, visit people, smile, explain Kenya ministry, visit people, preach, teach, visit people, speak, visit people.
Venue:	Sunday School classes, kitchens, churches, halls, restaurants, living rooms, cars, phone booths, etc.
Benefits:	Encouragement, encouragement, encouragement

Example Two - A Creative Furlough Newsletter

They came from Aargh!
They came from Ugh!
They came from beyond the galaxy.
All of them were alien, all of them were strange.
—*They Came From Aargh!* by Russell Hoban

The words from this children's book captured my thoughts after our reentry into the American culture. All of them were alien, all of them strange. We never thought we would feel like strangers in our own country, but during the past two months we have been continually reminded of how foreign the United States has become to us.

For example, during Katie's first week in American first grade, she kept scratching out all her mistakes instead of erasing them. Finally, Susan and I realized that she didn't know how to use an eraser. (In France she only used pens.) Katie also had to learn some English. Words like recess, principal and cafeteria were foreign to her. The rest of us have collided in our own ways with the American culture. Haley continues to kiss everyone on each cheek to greet them and Mackenzie keeps trying to teach her friends how to speak French. We find this particularly amusing since Mackenzie refused to speak the language when we lived in France.

And so la famille Lansing has crash-landed on planet American for a short stay before we make our big move to Zaire. In the two short months we have been here, we have already....

While on home ministry assignment, make a few phone calls to people who support you and thank them for their support. Keep it to a five or ten minute call. Leave a message of thanks if no one is home. Your donors will appreciate the personal touch! Another idea is to write a short personal note of appreciation.

Wholesale discount stores like Sam's Club and Costco, and department stores like Target or Walmart, offer long distance calling cards around three and a half to five cents per minute. With this, a ten-minute call becomes cheaper than sending a note!

Chapter Seven - Final Thoughts

One thing may help you the most.

Certainly you can create a newsletter that stimulates interest, prayer, world missions, and finances in God's kingdom work! But you must invest effort to write well.

Exceptional letters rarely just happen. With a hectic ministry, it is tempting to simply dump in the list of your activities and "get out a letter." Many missionaries do. I have a time or two. But when you skimp at writing well, it shows. Friends may not tell you, but they eventually stop reading your letters.

When I ask a missionary, "Tell me what is going on in your ministry," their eyes brighten and out flows interesting tales, predicaments, stories, and even struggles. Charles was no exception. He "lit up" while telling how God worked in non-religious students, motorcycle dudes, neighbors and family. I was hungry to listen to more! Yet when I read Charles' newsletters, those stories were missing.

Today a friend asked me, "What's going on in your ministry?" I excitedly gave an update and told a couple of stories. Then I realized *this is what a newsletter should do—tell stories about what God is doing as if you were asked!*

When you tell your stories, incorporate the tips in this book and captivate your readers. Don't settle for mediocre. Don't bore your readers. Write a great introduction. "Show" rather than "tell." Get feedback. Friends want to hear what is happening. Communicate the same spirit of love and grace Paul had toward the Philippians in these two verses: "I thank my God in all my remembrance of you…." "Now I want you to know…." (Philippians 1:3,12).

Thank you for serving the Lord Jesus Christ and giving Him the glory for His marvelous work. Indeed it is all about Him! Writing, learning and improving are ongoing areas of development and I welcome any thoughts or ideas you have too. My mentors taught me many of the tips in this book, and now I pass them on to you. Write, reap and rejoice!

APPENDIX

Checklist for Writing a Newsletter

Writing Tips for Exceptional Newsletters

- ☐ Include a Story
- ☐ Begin With a Bang
- ☐ Add a Picture and Caption
- ☐ Choose One Theme
- ☐ Use Appealing Graphics and Layout
- ☐ Write With Vitality
- ☐ Personalize It
- ☐ Get Feedback

Make a copy of this and use it as a checklist when writing your next newsletter.

Checklist for Editing and Proofing a Newsletter

CHECKLIST FOR EDITING AND PROOFING A NEWSLETTER

- ❑ Was anything confusing? Did you have to re-read any part of the letter?

- ❑ How could the letter flow better?

- ❑ Did the introduction draw you into the letter?

- ❑ Does the letter have one theme?

- ❑ Is there a short story?

- ❑ Are any words or terms confusing? Is there organizational jargon or lingo to clarify?

- ❑ Do any paragraphs need better transitions?

- ❑ What might illustrate the point better?

- ❑ Are there any typographical errors?

- ❑ Is the organizational logo included somewhere?

- ❑ Are the person's name and address listed?

- ❑ Is each letter personally signed?

- ❑ Is there a specific date?

- ❑ Does the picture(s) include a sentence caption?

- ❑ Is "thank you" stated?

Give a copy of this checklist to the person who is giving you feedback.

Checklist for Keeping Donors Once You Get Them

True or False? (answers at the bottom of the page)

_____ I must be close friends with everyone who supports my ministry.

_____ Generally, donors will keep investing in my ministry even if they never hear from me.

_____ Donors cheerfully invest in my ministry.

I. What is donor ministry? It is giving thanks and showing appreciation to your donors and keeping them informed. It also includes ministering to, serving, and giving to them.

II. Why is it important? It is biblical. Consider the verses below about the importance of communicating. Although you don't communicate solely for the income streams, the more you communicate with your donors, the more likely they will continue investing and praying. It strengthens friendships and is a way to express thanks.

Philippians 1:3-7 – "I thank my God in all my remembrance of you, always offering prayer with joy in my every prayer for you all, in view of your participation in the gospel…."

Philippians 4:10, 15-18 – "But I rejoiced in the Lord greatly, that now at last you have revived your concern for me; indeed, you were concerned before, but you lacked opportunity. And you yourselves also know…that at the first preaching of the gospel…no church shared with me in the matter of giving and receiving but you alone; …you sent a gift more than once for my needs. Not that I seek the gift itself, but I seek for the profit which increases to your account."

Romans 1:8-13 – "First, I thank my God through Jesus Christ for you all…For I long to see you…that I may be encouraged together with you while among you…."

I Corinthians 1:4 – "I thank my God always concerning you…."

2 Thessalonians 2:13 – "But we should always give thanks to God for you, brethren beloved by the Lord, because God has chosen you from the beginning for salvation through sanctification by the Spirit and faith in the truth."

"I am convinced that many donors stop giving because the missionary fails to say thank you."
—William Dillon, *People Raising*

III. How can I thank and inform my donors?

- ❑ Segment your mailing list and identify your regular givers as donors.
- ❑ Send your donors a letter (in addition to your newsletter) three to four times a year. Sample donor letters are in the appendix.
- ❑ Send one thank-you gift a year.
- ❑ Keep postcards, note cards, stamps and your addresses on hand (and while traveling). During pockets of free time, jot a few sentences and say thanks.
- ❑ Consider uses of e-mail.
- ❑ Have some personal contact once every year or two. This can be a five-minute phone call to say thanks, a short note, postcard, or a visit.
- ❑ Pray for your donors.
- ❑ Attend and serve at a supporting church mission's conference.
- ❑ Invite donors to conferences or local ministry events.
- ❑ If traveling through where donors live, stop by for a short visit (or phone call).

Answers: F, F, T

Examples of Donor Letters

Note: A supporting church may post your donor letter on a bulletin board for all to read, just like they would your newsletter. Keep that in mind if you include any personal or sensitive information in your letter.

Donor Letter Example 1

Logo
Date

Dear Support Team,

Thank you for your faithful support and prayer. You are a blessing, and we wanted to give you an update.

Shawn in Kuwait – I got a letter last week from Shawn. He is the young believer whom we featured in our last newsletter. He said, "Looks like we're getting some action. I'm glad I'm going in with God on my side…"

We also received a letter from another deployed Marine who said, "I know it's not easy to say, but in case the Lord calls me home, I've enclosed a letter that I want you to hold on to and give to my wife for me."

Katie – With her husband deployed, Katie decided to stay here locally until the summer. We are excited! She and Sandy get together weekly for encouragement, Bible study and learning practical ministry skills, like sharing her testimony. Today she said, "Thank you so much. One of my friends just asked me about my life. I want to tell her how I accepted Christ."

Car – Sandy's Nissan finally quit for good. The Lord allowed us to get a good deal on a Honda Accord, and it drives wonderfully. We are thankful.

Sad News – After seven weeks of pregnancy, Sandy miscarried last month. It was sad and very disappointing for us both, and we are up and down emotionally. I was sick with the flu when it happened, so it was a rough week for us both! Sandy's health has now recovered.

Cousin Sam's funeral service – My 44 year-old cousin Sam died unexpectedly in January. The family asked me to give the memorial service. It went well. Thanks for praying.

School of Infantry Bible Study – Because of your prayers and gifts, we have been able to start a Bible study for Marines fresh out of boot camp. My colleague Dave and I have seen 37 Marines attend, and Isaiah came to faith in Christ last week!

Though we have had some ups and downs, Sandy and I rejoice in Christ who is our life (Col. 3:4). We are days away from war with Iraq and want to ask you to pray these 14 prayer requests (enclosed) over the next 14 days. Thank you. We appreciate you!

Sharing His life,

Logo
Date

Dear Prayer and Support Team,

We appreciate your on-going support and prayers for this "ground-breaking" and "building" ministry in Venezuela. We are grateful for your investment. We love the peace and tranquility of life here. We enjoy beginning to reach new people on the campus and in the community. But we confess the "small town" mentality and slower pace have at times been frustrating. We want to give you an update and prayer request.

Luis and Sandra – One of the great privileges of coming to Venezuela is knowing Luis and Sandra. It all started about five years ago when Luis, a single guy and a new Christian at the time, shared the good news of Christ with his neighbors and good friends, Juan and Sandra. Shortly after coming to know Christ, they received the devastating news that Juan had a deadly form of cancer. He had only months to live. Juan had peace about going to heaven, but who would take care of Sandra and their two children? Juan called Luis to his bedside and told him that he believed it was God's will that Luis should marry his wife after his death!

Luis felt as if lightning had struck him! Could this possibly be? After Juan died, Luis and Sandra's friendship deepened and blossomed into love. They were later married and have been growing together as a family for three years now. God continues to use their lives.

Trinidad – We stay linked with Trinidad and travel there some. Our friends there continue to be very much part of our lives. The situation for Carlos in Trindad got worse, but in spite of that, he was able to share the Gospel with his entire gathering of family and friends! The Gospel is extending to places throughout Trinidad. Please continue to pray for Carlos and Ana. His work takes him all over the island.

The Home Front –
- Diane's parents are "wintering" with us in Venezuela.
- Joel is doing well at USNA. He has the days counted until the end of Plebe year!
- Don travels to New York for a meeting in March and will visit Joel too.
- Diane is back at school, this time as a student! She has been taking courses in Special Education and enjoys learning and making new friends.

Thanks for your wonderful concern and support.

Our love in Christ,

Logo

Date

Dear Giving Friends,

Many people know of William Carey, the "father of modern missions." But few people have heard of his sister. She was a quadriplegic and had to be carried from bed to couch. For 50 years she lay in bed and prayed for William Carey. She wrote him encouraging letters - with a pencil between her teeth.

Her ministry was perhaps more important because she was a *silent* partner. God knew. And certainly William Carey realized God's blessing was as much a result of his sister's commitment to his ministry as was his own dedication to serve God.

The same is true today. As missionaries, Tina and I know that our ministry would be impossible without giving and praying partners just like William Carey's sister. We need **YOU**. It is your *partnership* with us that makes ministry to the students of Indiana University possible.

I have a dream. I dream of seeing a band of students worshipping the Lord, praying to Him, eagerly looking for Him throughout all the Scriptures, humbling themselves before Him in brokenness over their pride and lukewarm devotion, waiting upon Him to fill them with His Spirit, serving Him with single-minded purpose and a passion that consumes all others. Laborers, **Christ-like** Laborers. This cannot happen apart from prayer and the work of God.

E. M. Bounds wrote, *God's promises lie like giant corpses without life, only for decay and dust, unless men appropriate and vivify these promises by earnest and prevailing prayer... Prayer honors God, acknowledges His being, exalts His power, adores His providence, secures His aid.* Jesus said it this way in John 15:5, *"...apart from me you can do nothing."* Would you pray for us? *Personally* - our own walk with the Lord. *Family* - to be what God wants. *Ministry* - pray that we would be able to reach and help the students God wants us to. (We will be doing many activities to recruit students at the beginning of the semester.)

Fall and the start of school will be here before you know it. I can already smell the excitement and apprehension of the freshmen as they move into the dorms for the first year of their college career. What an opportunity for the gospel!

In many ways I am like the freshmen coming in. I am both excited and apprehensive. The opportunities are endless but sometimes I become fearful and feel overwhelmed. I can be insecure and easily threatened by the task before me. Please pray for me to courageously trust God and to move out when needed.

Thanks for your thoughtfulness and for your gracious support. We appreciate **you**. Through your partnership, you stand with us on the front lines of reaching and discipling a hurting student world for Christ. Thank you!

Your missionaries at IU,

Logo

Date

Dear Friends,

A big smile came across my face when I received Kristen's call. I was in San Antonio at a conference and Katie was in Estes Park speaking at a woman's retreat but we were expecting to hear from her. With delight we'd like to announce that our daughter Kristen is engaged to Eric and will be married later this summer. We couldn't be more pleased!

It was almost 20 years ago while involved in student ministry at Penn State University that we would anticipate similar calls. Now we have our own graduate, Kristen, and also a college sophomore, Matthew at Colorado State University. Re-entering the collegiate ministry of The Navigators has brought back a flood of wonderful memories. Even though the years have slipped by, students still are desperate to hear of God's redeeming love. We count it a privilege to be a part of building His kingdom.

The reports we receive from our staff friends scattered across the country speak of a new openness and responsiveness to Christ and His gospel. One story comes from the first floor of Newsom Hall at Colorado State University. Every Monday night this fall a small band of students gather after dinner to read the Bible and watch Monday night football. Sometimes there is pizza—sometimes only a few come. Often the questions and discussion move in all directions, but Matt's room is a safe, inviting place to look into God's Word.

You can understand how excited we were a few weeks ago when with tears in his eyes Matt related that "Mike" had professed a faith in Christ! Whether in a small study or a conference attended by hundreds of students, this same story is unfolding on campuses all across the nation as students are loved and exposed to the good news of Christ. **Pray for God to bring forth an incredible harvest. Pray also for Matt's study, that God would draw each student to Himself!**

Katie and I are excited to have a part in what God is doing in the lives of young men and women who are seeking Him. Thank you for your friendship, prayers and financial support that allow us to be in the ministry of the gospel. Our prayer for you this Christmas season is that you will experience His love and safety in the coming year!

Rejoicing at His birth,

PS – Our Mike is enjoying his junior year in HS. Before you know it he will be off to college too!

Logo

Date

Dear Support Team,

By the time you receive this, I will be in southern Russia teaching English to Russian college students, and pointing them to Christ. Thank you for your support, prayers and concern. I'd like to give you an update and some prayer requests.

UPDATES:

- April *Finishers* conference in Dallas: this was for the "baby boomer" generation who are considering a second career in missions. I taught a workshop on "How hard is it to raise support?"

  Nearly a hundred people crowded into the workshop. The goal was to help them to see that raising support is possible, and biblical. A conference worker overhead this comment: *"It was exactly what we needed. She did not overwhelm us with all of the details, but showed it was possible and laid out a good beginning for us to think about this whole idea of fundraising."*

- New Staff Newsletter – This one-page motivator encourages, teaches and spurs momentum for over 60 new staff each year as they raise support for ministry. I have written and edited seven monthly issues and have five more to go.

- Home front – My roommate Jenny married Brad on June 3 at the Air Force Academy. It was a wonderful celebration and I shall miss them as they head to their first Air Force assignment. Ask God to bless them.

RUSSIA – PRAYER REQUESTS FOR SUMMER ENGLISH CAMP

- Acts 4:13 – "Now as they observed the confidence of Peter and John…they began to recognize them as having been with Jesus." Please pray that hundreds of Russians will be drawn to the reality of Christ in us.
- Excellence and good teamwork in teaching English
- Boldness, grace, friendships, encouraging believers, and the power of God to change lives.

Thank you for your support and love and concern. Yesterday I heard a report from a friend in Russia that there is a lot of openness to the gospel. I appreciate your partnership. It is exciting to serve with you in such a great adventure of helping build laborers for Russia and helping baby boomers learn about raising support and serving in missions. Thanks for helping make it all possible!

In His great love,

Logo

Date

Dear Giving Friends,

This letter comes to friends like you who have held the ropes for us in finances and prayer over the past 24 months. Thank you for your partnership. We wouldn't be in this work without you.

Whew! It's been a controlled whirlwind here since winter. Here are some highlights.

For thanksgiving:

- Launched our NAVevents. These Saturday 9 a.m. to 4 p.m. events are called "How to Experience God More Deeply." My Development team is joining with NavPress to pass on the Navigator values of experiencing God and living as an "insider." Seven more are lined up for next fall.

- Launched "Project Breakthrough." We are attempting to breakthrough with eight Navigator staff women to pave the way for women missionaries. Many staff women are setting their budgets too low simply to "get by." But this is not good for the long haul. They are committed to eight weeks of funding appeals this summer (deadline August 31).

For prayer:

- Please pray for my team and me as we appeal for four end-of-fiscal-year projects: National Leadership, Development, International Office, Glen Eyrie—total $(amount)! Pray that we will be able to make 50 key appeals by August 31. "I'm stretched!" Thanks.

- I speak to our New Staff Orientation June 2 on the biblical basis of funding their ministry. I do this about three times a year and look forward to it. Please pray that I would be able to meet the needs and that we would see changed lives.

Alma is well. Her ministry with the three Kathy's continues. Thanks for praying.

Yours in Christ,

Logo

Date

Dear Support Team,

Your gifts to our work in Uganda are making a difference! Thank you for your prayers and continued support. Here are two stories you will not here on CNN about God's work in Uganda.

- From a Ugandan worker: "You wouldn't believe it. Yesterday we were distributing food, Bibles and videos of 'JESUS' in an apartment building in Kampala. We went through the first three and ran out of food. So we decided to leave for home. Outside the building a woman came running after us. She said, 'Excuse me. You distributed these things to the other floors, but I am living on the fourth floor. I heard about it and you didn't give us anything!' We replied, 'We are sorry but we ran out of food.' She said 'No, I am not asking you for food. I want the film!'"

- Realizing that the doors are wide open in Uganda, a national staff leader from a nearby country recently took a risk and loaded his van with 10, 000 CDs of the children's version of the 'JESUS' film. This four-hour drive could be dangerous since others had been robbed along the way. When they departed they did not know if the soldiers at the border would confiscate the tapes or not.

As they approached the border checkpoint, they prayed. The checkpoint was jammed. When he tried to explain his cargo, the soldier became irritated. 'There are hundreds of cars behind you. Do you think I have time to investigate what is in your vehicle?" Get moving! Move along!' His only regret at the time was not bringing another 10,000 CDs that were left behind.

Please ask the Lord to use the 'JESUS' film and reach thousands of Ugandan children and families to plant seeds and reap belief in Him. Because of my knee surgery, I am not able to travel in-country with our team this year.

Pray too for wisdom in purchasing a newer car. My car has been in the shop three times this year and it is time for a replacement.

Thank you for your investment to bring His truth to the nations. I appreciate it!

Serving Him with You,

Fifty Ways of Saying "Thank You"
to your giving partners

1. I am excited that as you "honor the Lord from your wealth and from the first of all your produce," He will take care of you! And through your gifts, He is taking care of me too.
2. Thanks for your gift last month. It encouraged us.
3. It's a privilege to serve the Lord here in _____. Thanks for standing behind us.
4. I never get tired of thanking you for your support.
5. When David commissioned Solomon to build the house of the Lord, "the people rejoiced because they had offered so willingly and made their offering to the Lord with a whole heart...." I thank God for your willingness and wholeheartedness in giving.
6. It's a joy to serve Him in this ministry with you.
7. We are grateful for your gifts these past months. They have freed us to focus on training ten college students to share their faith.
8. I thought of the story of the widow in Luke 21 today and praised God that you also reach past your surplus to give to the Lord. Thanks for sharing it with me.
9. We rejoice that you faithfully supported us this past year. That means a lot to us.
10. Students at _____ are bombarded with pressure and opportunities to have sex without marriage. Your giving helps us reach them with the truth that only Jesus can satisfy our craving for genuine love. We value your partnership.
11. I am filled with thanks to the Father as you help supply my needs and make this ministry possible.
12. We praise God that you "do not neglect doing good and sharing." We appreciate how you share with us your gifts unto Him.
13. We often remember you in prayer and thank God for your part in our work.
14. I appreciate your readiness to give. Thanks.
15. Your giving is a ministry of His grace to us. Blessings to you.
16. You are a continual source of joy and encouragement to us as you pray and give so faithfully.
17. We thank God for you and pray that the Lord will "supply and multiply your seed for sowing and increase the harvest of your righteousness."
18. At our Bible study last night, _____ asked how he could know Jesus is God. Thanks for helping make it possible to reach businessmen like _____.
19. Each time your gift comes, I realize that your prayers back it up. That is such an encouragement!
20. The Lord overwhelms us with joy through your faithfulness to us.
21. Military personnel can search for fulfillment in the system, at the bars and in their performance. Thanks for helping me reach officers to show and tell them that Christ wants to be their Commanding Officer and their fulfillment.
22. It thrills me to receive your gifts these past months. May His grace be yours in abundance.
23. As Paul said to the Philippians, your gifts are "a fragrant offering, a sacrifice acceptable and pleasing to God."
24. Your prayers and gifts often cause me to praise God for His goodness.
25. Each month you bring a smile to my face as I see your gift. His blessings to you.
26. We appreciate your trust in God and decision to support us. We couldn't do it without friends like you.

27. I just returned from _____ where I taught how to help a new believer grow in Christ. Your support helped make this possible. Thanks for investing in raising up laborers for Christ.
28. You are a vital part of our lives and work.
29. Each time our monthly statement comes and we see your gift, we stop and thank the Lord for you!
30. What a pleasure to partner with you as God changes lives here in _____. Your gifts are touching lives, like _____. She understands more and more of the Gospel and is learning to trust. Thanks for your help!
31. We appreciate your friendship and partnership. We love you.
32. Often we are reminded of how precious you are to us. We appreciate you and your generous heart.
33. We feel such gratitude to the Lord for the way He touches hearts to be a part of this ministry. Thanks for your part!
34. As I write this, my heart is filled with gratitude for all you mean to me and helping make this ministry possible.
35. We realize you have choices where to give your money. Thanks for partnering with us in reaching _____ with the Gospel.
36. Thanks for standing behind me with your financial gifts. I feel honored and humbled.
37. Your prayers make a difference in our lives and work. And your faithful support is so helpful and encouraging. Hope you know what a joy you are to us.
38. It encourages me that you keep praying and giving.
39. We love you and are grateful for your partnership.
40. I am glad that the Lord brought you into my life and feel grateful for your continued support.
41. Your support makes it possible to serve the Lord in the task of _____. Thanks!
42. _____ and I feel humbled and glad that you are part of our support team. Many thanks!
43. You are truly partners with us in this work.
44. You are part of a team that "holds the ropes" for us while we go into inner city neighborhoods in _____. Your giving is a glorious gift to us!
45. You are storing up treasure in heaven as you give to the Lord through this ministry to _____ families.
46. As Hebrews 6:10 says, "God is not so unjust as to overlook your work, and the love which you showed for His sake in serving the saints, as you still do."
47. I appreciate your sacrifice to give so generously to this work.
48. Your gifts cheer our hearts and we praise Him for your partnership.
49. Thanks for standing with me in prayer and enabling me to disciple men like _____. He is beginning to understand his anger and see the Lord as his help.
50. I deeply appreciate you and your heart to give.

Sandy Buschman Weyeneth, The Navigators
Some material adapted from *Fifty Ways of Expressing Gratitude* by Ken Williams, Wycliffe Bible Translators

Bible Study on How a Thankful Spirit Transforms Newsletters

Few things wreck a newsletter like the tone of a missionary's ungrateful spirit. Most missionaries say they are thankful and think they communicate it. Many do an excellent job in expressing genuine thanks. However, over the years I discovered that more than a few missionaries dislike the hassle of newsletters. They are also secretly angry at having to raise support. It was true of me a few times. It sapped my thankfulness and made newsletters more of a duty than privilege.

Scriptures reveal volumes about our hearts and communicating thanks. A spirit of gratefulness can transform your newsletter more than you may realize. See how you rate. Take ten minutes and read the following verses. Mark the words and phrases showing thankfulness or praise.

I Chronicles 16:7	"Then on that day David first assigned Asaph and his relatives to give thanks to the Lord."
I Chronicles 29:11-13	"Thine, O Lord, is the greatness and the power and the glory and the victory and the majesty, indeed everything that is in the heavens and the earth; Thine is the dominion, O Lord, and Thou dost exalt Thyself as head over all. Both riches and honor come from Thee, and Thou dost rule over all, and in Thy hand is power and might; and it lies in Thy hand to make great, and to strengthen everyone. Now therefore, our God, we thank Thee, and praise Thy glorious name."
Psalm 95:2	"Let us come before His presence with thanksgiving; Let us shout joyfully to Him with psalms."
Psalm 100:4	"Enter His gates with thanksgiving, and His courts with praise. Give thanks to Him; bless His name.
Luke 17:12-19	"And as He entered a certain village, there met Him ten leprous men, who stood at a distance; and they raised their voices saying, 'Jesus, Master, have mercy on us!' And when He saw them, He said to them, 'Go and show yourselves to the priests.' And it came about that as they were going, they were cleansed. Now one of them, when he saw that he had been healed, turned back, glorifying God with a loud voice, and he fell on his face at His feet, giving thanks to Him. And he was a Samaritan. And Jesus answered and said, 'Were there not ten cleansed? But the nine—where are they? Were none found who turned back to give glory to God, except this foreigner?'"
Romans 1:8	"First, I thank my God through Jesus Christ for you all, because your faith is being proclaimed throughout the whole world."

I Corinthians 1:4	"I thank my God always concerning you, for the grace of God which was given you in Christ Jesus...."
II Corinthians 9:10-11	"Now He who supplies seed to the sower and bread for food, will supply and multiply your seed for sowing and increase the harvest of your righteousness; you will be enriched in everything for all liberality, which through us is producing thanksgiving to God."
I Corinthians 11:23-24	"For I received from the Lord that which I also delivered to you, that the Lord Jesus in the night in which He was betrayed took bread; and when He had given thanks, He broke it, and said, 'This is My body, which is for you; do this in remembrance of Me.'"
Philippians 4:6	"Be anxious for nothing, but in everything by prayer and supplication with thanksgiving let your requests be made known to God."
Philippians 1:3	"I thank my God in all my remembrance of you...."
Colossians 3:17	"And whatever you do in word or deed, do all in the name of the Lord Jesus, giving thanks through Him to God the Father."
1 Thessalonians 1:2	"We give thanks to God always for all of you, making mention of you in our prayers...."
I Thessalonians 5:16-18	"Rejoice always, pray without ceasing, in everything give thanks; for this is God's will for you in Christ Jesus."
2 Thessalonians 2:13	"But we should always give thanks to God for you, brethren beloved by the Lord, because God has chosen you from the beginning for salvation through sanctification by the Spirit and faith in the truth."
I Timothy 1:12	"I thank Christ Jesus our Lord, who has strengthened me, because He considered me faithful, putting me into service...."

Optional: Using a concordance, count how many times "thank(s)" and "thanksgiving" are mentioned in the Psalms. _____

Application: What may hinder my desire to be thankful?

In light of these verses, what attitude will I adopt about newsletters?

How can I communicate thankfulness in my newsletter?

REFERENCES

PAGE	SOURCE

6   Michelsen, Alvera. 1995. *How To Write Missionary Letters- Practical tips to make your words come alive, Revised seventh ed.* Media Associates International, Inc.

6   Dillon, William P. 1993. *People Raising – A Practical Guide To Raising Support.* Moody Press.

10   Colson, Charles. September 25, 2002. *Criticize by Creating – Art Within.* BreakPoint Online transcripts, a ministry of Prison Fellowship, No. 020925.

10   Hoyle, Glenn. July,1993. *What to say in your prayer letters.* Evangelical Missions Quarterly.

19   Jutkins, Ray. 2003. *Baker's Dozen: The 13 Platinum Most Fundamental Direct Marketing Creative Ideas.* Power Direct Marketing Online Newsletter, Rockingham-Jutkins Marketing.

19   *Pitney Bowes Press Release: Pitney Bowes Workplace Study Reveals Characteristics, Success Strategies of "High-Volume Messagers."* August 28, 2000. This is the fourth in a series of studies on Managing Communication in the 21st Century Workplace in partnership with The Institute for the Future, 2000. The study drew on ethnographic interviews or observational interviews, as well as extensive telephone surveys. The research was conducted between January and March 2000 and consisted of interviews with workers at all organizational levels in small, medium, large, and Fortune 500 companies in Canada, France, Germany, the United Kingdom and the United States of America.

19   Caples, John. 1974. *Tested Advertising Methods – Fourth ed.* Reward Books, Prentice-Hall, Inc.

28   Walker, Robert. 1985. *Leads and Story Openings.* Creation House.

30   Meier, Dave. January 27,2003. Personal letter from corporate trainer regarding adult learning styles. Lake Geneva, Wis.: Founder of The Center For Accelerated Learning.

30   Morton, Scott. 1999. *Funding Your Ministry – Whether You're Gifted or Not!* Dawson Media—a ministry of The Navigators.

34   Coffman, Carrie Sydnor. 1991. *Bored Readers Don't Pray Much.* Apples of Gold, 1991.

34   Morton, Scott. 1999. *Funding Your Ministry.*

48   Barnett, Betty. 1991. *Friend Raising – Building a Support Team That Lasts.* YWAM Publishing—a division of Youth With A Mission.

49   Beach, Mark. 1988. *Editing Your Newsletter – How to Produce an Effective Publication Using Traditional Tools and Computers, Third ed.* Coast to Coast Books.

49   Morton, Scott. 1999. *Funding Your Ministry.*

50   Beach, Mark. 1993. *Newsletter Sourcebook.* North Light Books.

54   Beach, Mark. 1993. *Newsletter Sourcebook.*

54   Beach, Mark. 1988. *Editing Your Newsletter.*

55 Rubin, Jeff. Website newsletter, printed 2003. *Newsletter Design & Writing Tips.* Pinole, CA: Editor/owner, Put It In Writing Newsletter Publishers.

57 Zinsser, William. 1985.*On Writing Well – An informal guide to writing nonfiction, Third ed.* Harper and Row, Publishers, Inc.

58 Nichols, Sue. 1963. *Words on Target – For Better Christian Communication.* John Knox Press.

60 Eggenschwiler, Jean and Emily Dotson Biggs. 2001. *CliffsQuickReview Writing: Grammar, Usage, and Style.* Hungry Minds, Inc.

61 Wienbroer, Diana Roberts et al. 2000. *Rules of Thumb For Business Writers, Fourth ed.* McGraw-Hill.

66 Eggenschwiler, Jean and Emily Dotson Biggs. 2001. *CliffsQuickReview..*

66 Strunk Jr., William and E.B. White. 2000 *The Elements of Style, Fourth ed.* Longman Publishers.

82 Morton, Scott. 1999. *Funding Your Ministry.*

88 United States Postal Service. June 2003. *A Guide to Mailing for Businesses and Organizations.*

94 *Say It with E-mail.* May 22, 2000. Business Week, p. 62. Report on a study conducted by the Pew Research Center.

96 *Pitney Bowes Press Release*: *Connected Households Still Prefer Regular Mail.* April 3, 2001. Based on a survey conducted by the ICR Research Group. The survey was conducted by phone to 1,009 U.S. households, and it determined that 53 percent of those surveyed have access to e-mail at home. The statistics included in this release are based on that 53 percent.

96 *Pitney Bowes Press Release: From the Curbside Mailbox, With Love New Study Reveals Americans Remain Committed to Traditional Mail Despite the Lure of E-mail.* June 22, 2000. Based on a survey conducted by ICR Research Group. The survey was conducted by phone to 509 households across the continental United States. Of the respondents, 60 percent had access to an e-mail account either at home or through their work place.

97 Fryer, Bronwyn. July 1, 1999. *E-Mail: Backbone of the Info Age or Smoking Gun?* Your Company, v9 i5 p73+.

97 DiSabatino, Jennifer. February 5, 2001. *Don't Blame E-Mail.* Computerworld, p. 38.

101 Michelsen, Alvera. 1995. *How To Write Missionary Letters.*

RESOURCES

WRITING RESOURCES

Bored Readers Don't Pray Much, Carrie Sydnor Coffman, Apples of Gold, 1991.
CliffsQuickReview, Writing: Grammar, Usage, and Style, Jean Eggenschwiler and Emily Dotson Biggs, Hungry Minds, Inc., 2001.
The Elements of Style, William Strunk Jr.and E.B. White, Macmillan Publishing Co., Inc., 1979.
The First Five Pages – A Writer's Guide to Staying Out of the Rejection Pile, Noah Lukeman, Simon & Schuster, 2000.
How To Write Missionary Letters – Practical tips to make your words come alive, Alvera Michelsen, Media Associates International, 1995.
Leads and Story Openings, Robert Walker, Creation House, 1985.
On Writing Well – An informal guide to writing nonfiction, William Zinsser, Harper and Row, 1985.
Rules of Thumb For Business Writers, Fourth ed., Diana Roberts et al, McGrall-Hill, 2000.
Words on Target – For Better Christian Communication, Sue Nichols, John Knox Press, 1963.

DESIGN RESOURCES

Editing Your Newsletter – How to Produce an Effective Publication Using Traditional Tools and Computers, Mark Beach, Coast to Coast Books, 1988.
Newsletter Sourcebook, Mark Beach, North Light Books, 1993.
Principles, Pitfalls & Pizzazz, Carolyn Andrews, Designer Bytes Publications, 1994.

FUNDRAISING RESOURCES

Cash Project Appeals – Writing Appeal Letters for Your Ministry Projects, Sandy Buschman (Editor), The Navigators Staff Funding Team, 1996; P.O. Box 6000, Colorado Springs, CO 80934 USA.
Friend Raising – Building a Support Team That Lasts, Betty Barnett, YWAM Publishing—a division of Youth With A Mission, 1991; P.O. Box 55787, Seattle, WA 98155 USA.

Funding Your Ministry – Whether You're Gifted or Not! Scott Morton, Dawson Media—a ministry of The Navigators, 1999; P.O. Box 6000, Colorado Springs, CO 80934 USA, www.dawsonmedia.org.
People Raising – A Practical Guide to Raising Support, William P. Dillon, Moody Press, 1993; Chicago, IL 60610 USA.

OTHER RESOURCES

A Guide to Mailing for Businesses and Organizations, United States Postal Service, June 2003.
The Center For Accelerated Learning. Dave Meier, corporate trainer, Lake Geneva, WI; www.alcenter.com.

Envelope Sealer – This "besSeal Envelope Sealer" (Model 1000) is easy to use. You run each envelope through by hand, and you can seal up to 30 envelopes a minute. Order at:
Besline Corporation
P.O. Box "D," Tri-Cities, WA 99302
509/545-8062
800/237-7325
509/545-9240 (fax)

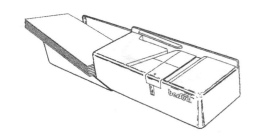

NEWSLETTER AND MAILING SERVICES

BMC Letter Service
P.O. Box 3234
Ft. Smith, AR 72913-3234
479/785-0262
479/785-1060 (fax)
www.bmcletterservice.com
bmc@bmcletterservice.com

BMC (named for founders Bob and Marie Canaday) is a letter service that prints and mails prayer letters for missionaries around the world. They are capable of downloading newsletters from a variety of software programs and for a variety of types of newsletters.

Mission Center International
Attn: Deana Spyres
PO Box 104
Beggs, OK 74421-0104
918/850-6326
918/ 267-5224
918/ 267-5224 (fax)
www.missioncenterintl.com
missioncenter@earthlink.net

MCI has provided missionaries, churches and religious organizations a timely, low cost newsletter printing and mailing service worldwide since 1972. MCI is a non-profit organization harnessing advanced technology with biblical precepts to prosper the family of God. Using the newest in high tech computers, printing, inserting and addressing equipment, the staff produces and mails your materials in ten days or less.

CRISTA Letter Service
19303 Fremont Ave. North
Mailstop #69
Seattle, WA 98133
206/546-7313
206/546-7317 (fax)
letterservice@crista.net

CRISTA Letter Service is a CRISTA Ministry—a Christian nonprofit organization. CRISTA Letter Service processes and sends your newsletters to your mailing list so you can focus on ministry. They offer full color and/or black and white services and also produce postcards, brochures, response cards, inserts and more. CRISTA strives to generate a quality product in a timely manner, for a minimal investment, as it has for nearly 50 years. They use Publisher, PageMaker and Word to format letters and can receive your input by mail or e-mail.

Mailers Club
3322 Garfield Ave.
Los Angeles, CA 90040
866/327-8624
323-722-2042
323/722-6774 (fax)
www.mailersclub.com
sales@mailersclub.com

An internet-based service offering a fast and easy way to print and send mail. You provide the mailing list and mailer content and in just a few days they print, fold, stuff, seal, address, add postage and deliver your entire mailing to the post office. They can mail to any country in the world.